INTRODUCING
ISSUES WITH
OPPOSING
VIEWPOINTS®

Privacy

Lauri S. Scherer, *Book Editor*

GREENHAVEN PRESS

A part of Gale, Cengage Learning

GALE
CENGAGE Learning®

Farmington Hills, Mich • San Francisco • New York • Waterville, Maine
Meriden, Conn • Mason, Ohio • Chicago

Elizabeth Des Chenes, *Director, Content Strategy*
Cynthia Sanner, *Publisher*
Douglas Dentino, *Manager, New Product*

For more information, contact:
Greenhaven Press
27500 Drake Rd.
Farmington Hills, MI 48331-3535
Or you can visit our Internet site at gale.cengage.com

For product information and technology assistance, contact us at

Gale Customer Support, 1-800-877-4253
For permission to use material from this text or product, submit all requests online at www.cengage.com/permissions

Further permissions questions can be e-mailed to permissionrequest@cengage.com

Articles in Greenhaven Press anthologies are often edited for length to meet page require-ments. In addition, original titles of these works are changed to clearly present the main thesis and to explicitly indicate the author's opinion. Every effort is made to ensure that Greenhaven Press accurately reflects the original intent of the authors. Every effort has been made to trace the owners of copyrighted material.

Cover image © Vasin Lee/Shutterstock.com.

LIBRARY OF CONGRESS CATALOGING-IN-PUBLICATION DATA

Privacy / Lauri S. Scherer, book editor.
    pages cm. -- (Introducing issues with opposing viewpoints)
  Summary: "IIOVP: Privacy: This title considers the state of privacy, the relationship between privacy and security, and the relationship between privacy and technology"--Provided by publisher.
  Includes bibliographical references and index.
  ISBN 978-0-7377-6927-2 (hardback)
1. Privacy, Right of--United States--Juvenile literature. 2. National security--United States--Juvenile literature. 3. Electronic surveillance--United States--Juvenile literature.
I. Scherer, Lauri S.
  JC596.2.U5P758 2014
  323.44'80973--dc23
                              2014003030

Printed in the United States of America
1 2 3 4 5 6 7 18 17 16 15 14

Contents

Foreword

Indulging in a wide spectrum of ideas, beliefs, and perspectives is a critical cornerstone of democracy. After all, it is often debates over differences of opinion, such as whether to legalize abortion, how to treat prisoners, or when to enact the death penalty, that shape our society and drive it forward. Such diversity of thought is frequently regarded as the hallmark of a healthy and civilized culture. As the Reverend Clifford Schutjer of the First Congregational Church in Mansfield, Ohio, declared in a 2001 sermon, "Surrounding oneself with only like-minded people, restricting what we listen to or read only to what we find agreeable is irresponsible. Refusing to entertain doubts once we make up our minds is a subtle but deadly form of arrogance." With this advice in mind, Introducing Issues with Opposing Viewpoints books aim to open readers' minds to the critically divergent views that comprise our world's most important debates.

Introducing Issues with Opposing Viewpoints simplifies for students the enormous and often overwhelming mass of material now available via print and electronic media. Collected in every volume is an array of opinions that captures the essence of a particular controversy or topic. Introducing Issues with Opposing Viewpoints books embody the spirit of nineteenth-century journalist Charles A. Dana's axiom: "Fight for your opinions, but do not believe that they contain the whole truth, or the only truth." Absorbing such contrasting opinions teaches students to analyze the strength of an argument and compare it to its opposition. From this process readers can inform and strengthen their own opinions, or be exposed to new information that will change their minds. Introducing Issues with Opposing Viewpoints is a mosaic of different voices. The authors are statesmen, pundits, academics, journalists, corporations, and ordinary people who have felt compelled to share their experiences and ideas in a public forum. Their words have been collected from newspapers, journals, books, speeches, interviews, and the Internet, the fastest growing body of opinionated material in the world.

Introducing Issues with Opposing Viewpoints shares many of the well-known features of its critically acclaimed parent series, Opposing Viewpoints. The articles are presented in a pro/con format, allowing readers to absorb divergent perspectives side by side. Active reading questions preface each viewpoint, requiring the student to approach the material thoughtfully and carefully. Useful charts, graphs, and cartoons supplement each article. A thorough introduction provides readers with crucial background on an issue. An annotated bibliography points the reader toward articles, books, and websites that contain additional information on the topic. An appendix of organizations to contact contains a wide variety of charities, nonprofit organizations, political groups, and private enterprises that each hold a position on the issue at hand. Finally, a comprehensive index allows readers to locate content quickly and efficiently.

Introducing Issues with Opposing Viewpoints is also significantly different from Opposing Viewpoints. As the series title implies, its presentation will help introduce students to the concept of opposing viewpoints and learn to use this material to aid in critical writing and debate. The series' four-color, accessible format makes the books attractive and inviting to readers of all levels. In addition, each viewpoint has been carefully edited to maximize a reader's understanding of the content. Short but thorough viewpoints capture the essence of an argument. A substantial, thought-provoking essay question placed at the end of each viewpoint asks the student to further investigate the issues raised in the viewpoint, compare and contrast two authors' arguments, or consider how one might go about forming an opinion on the topic at hand. Each viewpoint contains sidebars that include at-a-glance information and handy statistics. A Facts About section located in the back of the book further supplies students with relevant facts and figures.

Following in the tradition of the Opposing Viewpoints series, Greenhaven Press continues to provide readers with invaluable exposure to the controversial issues that shape our world. As John Stuart Mill once wrote: "The only way in which a human being can make some approach to knowing the whole of a subject is by hearing what can be said about it by persons of every variety of opinion and studying all modes in which it can be looked at by every character of mind. No wise man ever acquired his wisdom in any mode but this." It is to this principle that Introducing Issues with Opposing Viewpoints books are dedicated.

Introduction

Privacy—particularly how it should be protected in a digital context—is among one of the most discussed and debated topics of our time. Yet interestingly, the law that governs how authorities can legally access digital communications is nearly three decades old. That technology has outpaced the laws governing its legal protection has proven complicated and problematic for law enforcement officials; companies like Google, Facebook, and Yahoo; and citizens who want their communications to be private.

The Electronic Communications Privacy Act (ECPA) makes it legal for authorities to access e-mail or other messages that are stored on a third party's server for more than 180 days without a warrant or other form of judicial review. The material is considered "abandoned" after this roughly six-month period, and thus all that is required for authorities to access it is a written statement saying the information contained therein is needed for an investigation.

The difficulty is that this law was written in 1986. At that time, e-mail—which was not widely used by the general population—was not usually stored for such a length of time. Today, of course, users of web-based e-mail accounts like Gmail or Yahoo store e-mail for months or years, never deleting content because of constantly growing free storage limits and because it is often convenient to access a library of older e-mails. In addition, posts to social media websites remain on the companies' servers indefinitely, and a main purpose of cloud-based platforms that store documents, photos, videos, and other content on third-party servers is to be able to access them wherever a user may be, with no time limit or expiration date.

Should such content be downloaded and stored on a person's computer, it would be subject to warrant, no matter how old. But if such data are stored on a server, no warrant is needed after the content is 180 days old. Therefore, given the way in which people increasingly access their digital communications—via cell phone, tablet, cloud-based platform, or other mobile-friendly medium—the majority of people's digital communications are accessible to authorities with no warrant or other judicial review, which is a big problem for privacy advocates.

The American Civil Liberties Union (ACLU) is among many organizations that think the ECPA must be updated to catch up with contemporary digital realities. "In 1986, there was no World Wide Web, nobody carried a cell phone, and the only 'social networking' two-year-old [Facebook founder] Mark Zuckerberg was doing was at pre-school or on play dates," the ACLU points out. "Like the DeLorean [time-travel car] of [the movie] 'Back to the Future,' most of these technologies were still the stuff of sci-fi fantasies in 1986."[1] The tech company Intel agrees and argues that the law has fallen too far behind modern-day technologies that are part and parcel of today's basic communications methods. "ECPA was designed to deal with the technology of a 1986 world, where cell phones cost thousands of dollars and were the size of bricks, the Internet was confined to a handful of labs and military facilities, and GPS technology was not really publicly available," wrote Intel bloggers on the ECPA's twenty-fifth anniversary. "Happy Birthday, ECPA! Sorry to say, but you're looking pretty old."[2]

The ACLU, Intel, and other companies and organizations that do not usually join forces to take a position on a social issue like privacy have urged Congress to update the ECPA to better protect citizens' privacy. They have demanded that all personal electronic information be covered by the law, regardless of whether it has been downloaded to a personal computer or is accessible via a third-party platform or server. They also think government officials should be required to obtain a warrant to access information transmitted by cell phones and other mobile devices. According to the organization Digital Due Process, which was created by a diverse coalition of companies, think tanks, and public-interest groups with a vested interest in updating the ECPA,

> Information should receive the same protection regardless of technology or platform. Reform should preserve the building blocks of criminal investigations—subpoenas, court orders, etc.—as well as the sliding scale that allows law enforcement to escalate investigations. Generally, a type of information should have the same level of protection whether it is in transit or being stored. How old a communication is—or whether or not it has been opened—should be irrelevant to the privacy protections it receives.[3]

However, others warn that updating the ECPA will hamper intelligence investigations, facilitate criminal activity, and make it more difficult for authorities to apprehend terrorists. Cutting authorities off from such information or requiring them to first obtain a warrant to access it, could jeopardize the numerous intelligence investigations that rely on covert surveillance to succeed. For this reason, law enforcement agencies and criminal justice experts have argued that expanding protection of digital communication impedes authorities' access to crucial information that makes the fight against terrorism even more difficult than it already is. "When your job is to protect us by fighting and prosecuting crime, you want every tool available," explains Ryan Calo, director of the consumer privacy project at the Center for Internet and Society at Stanford Law School. Calo argues that authorities do not make these requests for nefarious reasons but because there is a legitimate investigative need. "No one thinks [the] D.O.J. [Department of Justice] and other investigative agencies are sitting there twisting their mustache trying to violate civil liberties," says Calo. "They're trying to do their job."[4]

In April 2013, the Senate Judiciary Committee sought to address this issue when it approved legislation known as S. 607 that, if passed into law, would amend the ECPA in some of the ways recommended by these advocacy organizations. Also known as the Leahy-Lee Electronic Communications Privacy Act Amendments Act of 2013, S. 607 proposes that search warrants be required for all electronic communications stored by a third-party provider. It would also require authorities to notify the owners of the e-mails, within ten days of obtaining the warrant, that their communications have been accessed. The act's introduction was notable for its bipartisan support; it was cosponsored by Democratic senator from Vermont Patrick Leahy and Republican senator from Utah Mike Lee. "All Americans—regardless of political party affiliation or ideology—care about their privacy rights,"[5] said Leahy, who was an author of the original 1986 law. "Reforming ECPA to protect legitimate privacy rights is not a partisan issue,"[6] added Lee. The act was yet to be debated by Congress as of this writing.

The extent to which electronic communications should be private, whether the government should need a warrant to access them, and how best to protect privacy in the digital age are among the key issues debated in *Introducing Issues with Opposing Viewpoints: Privacy.* Through carefully selected viewpoints, students will consider the state of privacy, the importance of privacy, the relationship between privacy and security, the relationship between technology and privacy, and other critical issues pertaining to this ever more important topic.

Notes

1. American Civil Liberties Union, "Modernizing the Electronic Communications Privacy Act (ECPA)," 2013. www.aclu.org /technology-and-liberty/modernizing-electronic-communications -privacy-act-ecpa.
2. Intel Blog Administrator, "Happy 25th Birthday, ECPA! It's Time for a Refresh," *Policy@Intel* (blog), Intel.com, October 21, 2011. http://blogs.intel.com/policy/2011/10/21/happy_25th_birthday _ecpa_its_time_for_a_refresh.
3. Center for Democracy & Technology, "Security and Surveillance," 2013. www.cdt.org/issue/wiretap-ecpa.
4. Quoted in Miguel Helft and Claire Cain Miller, "1986 Privacy Law Is Outrun by Web," *New York Times,* January 9, 2011. www.nytimes .com/2011/01/10/technology/10privacy.html?pagewanted=all.
5. Patrick Leahy, "SJC Approves Leahy-Lee Electronic Communications Privacy Amendments Act," Leahy senatorial website, April 25, 2013. www.leahy.senate.gov/press/sjc-approves-leahy-lee-electronic-com munications-privacy-amendments-act-.
6. Quoted at Leahy, "SJC Approves Leahy-Lee Electronics Communications Privacy Amendments Act."

Chapter 1

What Is the State of Privacy?

Privacy, on computers and in person, has become a hot topic in today's political landscape.

Privacy

Privacy is the a
group to seclud
nformation abo
rereby reveal t
e boundaries
nsidered priva
d individuals

Viewpoint 1

Privacy Is Dead

Andrew Lam

Privacy is dead, warns Andrew Lam in the following viewpoint. Lam claims the terrorist attacks of September 11, 2001, heralded an era in which Americans became increasingly willing to trade their privacy for increased security. Americans are now used to having low expectations of privacy in airports and in certain kinds of communications and even prefer to give up some elements of privacy if they think it will help authorities keep them safe, the author contends. In addition to safety, Lam asserts that the advent of social media has encouraged Americans to violate their own privacy—people willingly share personal information online with no care about whether it is appropriate to do so. If Americans are not careful, argues Lam, they will soon find themselves living in a society in which no one has any privacy, which he thinks would be disastrous.

Lam is the web editor for New American Media, a multimedia ethnic news agency.

> *"#Privacy is not to be had, #imsorry tosay."*

Andrew Lam, "Privacy Is Lost, and We Are All to Blame," TruthOut.org, July 5, 2013. Reproduced with permission.

AS YOU READ, CONSIDER THE FOLLOWING QUESTIONS:
1. What is PRISM, as described by Lam?
2. As reported by the author, what percentage of Americans surveyed said that government spying programs help prevent terrorist attacks?
3. In what specific ways do businesses track individuals, according
to Lam?

W hen full-body scanners were introduced at American airports three years ago [in 2010], there was a brief public outcry. But just as quickly, it died down. Travelers
interviewed shrugged off the loss of privacy in the name of safety,
using terms like "trade-off" and "compromise." One frequent trav-
eler seemed to sum up the general attitude when he said he'd grown
"immune to the procedures."

In other words, Americans don't want to be groped or scanned,
don't want our personal spaces invaded, but we're willing to endure
both in the name of security. Such is the contract between the people
and the state in the new, post-9/11 America.

The Increased Willingness to Give Away Rights

At airports, it is understood that you're not allowed to exercise your
rights—the Second Amendment explicitly and the First implicitly.
It's common sense that you don't ever carry a gun on a plane. And
since 9/11, don't even think of saying the word "bomb" to a TSA
[Transportation Security Administration] agent, even if it's a joke.
Travelers have been routinely detained for doing just that. Passengers
have even been kicked off planes for wearing t-shirts that were deemed
offensive. One passenger was removed for wearing a shirt with an
Arabic inscription that said, ironically, "We Will Not Be Silent." He
later sued Jet Blue and the two TSA screeners and won.

How you dress and what you say can be used against you at airports, where scanners and cameras and security guards are aplenty,
and where you are constantly being monitored.

But what if, in the name of security, you were willing to give up
more rights, not just at the airport, but everywhere else? What if the

The terrorist attacks of September 11, 2001, heralded an era in which Americans became increasingly willing to trade their privacy for increased security.

whole country were to slowly become a kind of mega-airport, a place where you had to watch your language and restrict your communication activities, all under the watchful, electronic eye of Uncle Sam?

That is increasingly becoming the scenario in America today, as the story of Edward Snowden versus the National Security Agency [NSA] unfolds.

Resignation Where There Should Be Outrage

Snowden blew the whistle on PRISM, a government program that collects enormous amounts of data from the phone and Internet records of Americans, as well as others living outside of the U.S. Though PRISM's existence has been known about for years, the sheer amount of data being mined is revelatory—3 billion pieces of intelligence were culled from the computer networks of U.S. residents in March of 2013 alone.

Snowden is now on the run from authorities in the U.S., who want him tried for treason.

But even as Americans worry that their personal communication records are being monitored without their consent, many say that the spying works as a deterrent for terrorism attacks, according to a recent *USA Today*/Pew Research poll. Americans surveyed were more or less split (48 to 47 percent) on whether they approve or disapprove of such programs as part of the nation's anti-terrorism effort. Yet, more than half (53 percent) of those surveyed also said government spying programs help prevent terrorist attacks. And a slight majority (54 percent) felt that Snowden should be criminally prosecuted.

> ## FAST FACT
>
> In 2008 a Pennsylvania couple sued Google Street View (part of Google Maps) for taking and posting photos of their house, despite the "private property" signs. Google argued that twenty-first-century satellite-imaging technology invalidates the notion of complete privacy. Google was ordered to pay only a dollar in damages.

Overall, instead of outrage there's a feeling of resignation in the air, as the story of Snowden versus the NSA unfolds. On twitter, the resignation often manifests as humor:

#NSACalledToTellMe What Happens in Vegas, stays in our Utah data center.

#NSACalledToTellMe that next time a politician says "I am listening to YOU" they really mean it.

We can hear you now. #NSACalledToTellMe

The Altered Notion of Privacy

Part of the problem is that privacy isn't what it once was. Diaries once kept locked in one's drawer have become blogs for all to see. The domestic doings of private citizens are often captured in the raw on YouTube and Vimeo, as if their lives are reality TV shows. If Americans are wary that we are being constantly monitored, we, too, are guilty of divulging our secrets—we make spying on us an easy task. Between our urge to tweet opinions, our impulse to photograph meals on Instagram, our need to share every sorrow and update our every move on Facebook, we have more or less become an open book. In essence, we volunteer information about ourselves as habit. And the way technology is going, with social media increasingly becoming an integral part of our daily communication, #privacy is not to be had, #imsorrytosay.

Spying, too, is no longer the business of government agencies. Increasingly, tracking is done not by various companies and organizations but by individuals. Shopping malls monitor your shopping patterns by tracking your cell phone. Advertisers target individuals based on their interests, a seemingly personal touch accomplished by sophisticated, impersonal software. Self-tracking, too, is increasing. There are wireless devices that can track people's physical activities, while other devices can measure brainwave activity at night to chart people's sleep patterns online. And as drones are becoming smaller and smaller, it is only a matter of time before feuding neighbors or distrusting spouses can spy on one another using this technology, a kind of [movie spies] Mr. and Mrs. Smith writ large.

The New Norm

Privacy issues aside, in the post 9/11 era Americans live with a new set of norms. Mass deportation of undocumented immigrants who toil on our land has become the new norm, and despite talks of reform, those without proper papers continue to get swept up in wide sweeping government dragnets. The new norm allows careful surveillance of Muslim communities and many don't mention certain words like "jihad" or "bomb" on the phone, out of fear it might trigger investigation. Since they are being heavily monitored, some Arab Americans have invented roundabout ways to refer to their own children or relatives who have common names [like the notorious Osama bin Laden (the leader of

"Of course, I expect all this to remain strictly private!," cartoon by Mike Keefe, *Denver Post*, Cagle Cartoons, May 26, 2010. Copyright © 2010 by Mike Keefe and Cagle Cartoons.

al Qaeda, which attacked the United States in 2001) and Saddam Hussein (Iraqi president executed for crimes against humanity)].

Abroad, this new norm allows the U.S. to wage war overseas in perpetuity, in the name of national security, and with the right to preemptive strikes. We have accepted torture in the form of waterboarding, and the practice of kidnapping foreign citizens for interrogation (we call it extraordinary rendition), all while our drones in the sky routinely assassinate potential enemies and innocent victims who just happened to end up in our target range (we call them "collateral damage.")

The new norm also keeps our so-called "enemy combatants" in an offshore prison named Guantanamo and refuses their human rights and due process. In essence, they are serving life sentences without trials. When they go on hunger strikes, they are force-fed.

So is Snowden a hero or a traitor? On the one hand, by taking classified information that could harm the U.S. and then fleeing abroad—to Hong Kong, then Russia—he seems less heroic than self-preserving, especially for someone who says they want to bring about social change. (By contrast, [Vietnam War] whistle blower Daniel Ellsberg of Pentagon Papers fame stuck around and dealt with the consequences.) On the other hand, Snowden made Americans look at something from which we had learned to look away—internal government procedures to which we feel immune, until those procedures are spelled out in stark and dreadful terms, and we don't like what we see.

Hear the Wake Up Call

Every generation needs to grapple with and find the balance between national security and civil liberties, now more than ever. Democracy, after all, cannot possibly survive when the citizenry continues to cow behind draconian policies that override civil liberties in the name of the war on terror.

That Snowden pulled back the curtain and showed us the inner workings of the spy machinery should be a wake up call. But for now, that doesn't seem to be the case. In Dante's divine comedy there is a phrase that [is] inscribed above the gate of hell that says, "Abandon all hope, ye who enter here." If you replace the word "hope" with "rights" it could be hung above the entrances of American airports. What's worrisome is that as more and more Americans weigh in on the side of safety over civil liberties, that phrase might end up hanging above the Exit signs.

EVALUATING THE AUTHOR'S ARGUMENTS:

To make his argument, viewpoint author Andrew Lam argues that Americans participate in eroding their own privacy when they overshare via social media. How might Danah Boyd, author of the following viewpoint, respond to this argument? Summarize her likely position in two to three sentences, then state your opinion on this issue—do social media critically threaten privacy? Why or why not?

Privacy Is
Not Dead

Danah Boyd

*"People will
not abandon
social media,
nor will
privacy
disappear."*

In the following viewpoint Danah Boyd argues that privacy is not dead. She agrees that social media have challenged the way people regard privacy but contends that social media do not challenge privacy any more than real life does. People have just not yet adapted to balancing privacy with using social media. People are used to managing their privacy as they navigate the real world, she maintains—they lower their voices when speaking about sensitive matters, ask people to keep information private, and do not tell others what they do not want them to know. Boyd contends that people have not yet learned to manage online interactions according to these same guidelines but predicts that they soon will. Boyd also argues that social media software should be designed to better reflect people's natural, real-world sense of privacy. She concludes that privacy is not dead; it just needs to master the transition to online spaces.

Boyd is a social-media researcher at Microsoft Research New England and a fellow at Harvard University's Berkman Center for Internet and Society.

Danah Boyd, "Why Privacy Is Not Dead," *MIT Technology Review*, August 25, 2010. Reproduced with permission.

AS YOU READ, CONSIDER THE FOLLOWING QUESTIONS:
1. What does Erving Goffman, as cited by Boyd, call not listening to other people's conversations?
2. What does the author offer as an example of a privacy fail?
3. What, according to Boyd, must people develop if they are to communicate appropriately via Twitter and Facebook?

Each time Facebook's privacy settings change or a technology makes personal information available to new audiences, people scream foul. Each time, their cries seem to fall on deaf ears.

The reason for this disconnect is that in a computational world, privacy is often implemented through access control. Yet privacy is not simply about controlling access. It's about understanding a social context, having a sense of how our information is passed around by others, and sharing accordingly. As social media mature, we must rethink how we encode privacy into our systems.

Cultivating Privacy in Real Life

Privacy is not in opposition to speaking in public. We speak privately in public all the time. Sitting in a restaurant, we have intimate conversations knowing that the waitress may overhear. We count on what [sociologist] Erving Goffman called "civil inattention": people will politely ignore us, and even if they listen they won't join in, because doing so violates social norms. Of course, if a close friend sits at the neighboring table, everything changes. Whether an environment is public or not is beside the point. It's the situation that matters.

Whenever we speak in face-to-face settings, we modify our communication on the basis of cues

> **FAST FACT**
>
> According to Pew Research surveys in 2012, most Americans still value their privacy: 86 percent have taken steps to avoid being tracked online, 54 percent have decided not to install a cell phone app because it asked for personal data, and 60 percent of teens set their Facebook profiles to private (visible by friends only).

Before people can communicate appropriately in an online environment like Facebook or Twitter, they must develop a sense of how and what people share in person, the author argues.

like who's present and how far our voices carry. We negotiate privacy explicitly—"Please don't tell anyone"—or through tacit understanding. Sometimes, this fails. A friend might gossip behind our back or fail to understand what we thought was implied. Such incidents make us question our interpretation of the situation or the trustworthiness of the friend.

Developing a Sense of Online Privacy

All this also applies online, but with additional complications. Digital walls do almost have ears; they listen, record, and share our messages. Before we can communicate appropriately in a social environment like Facebook or Twitter, we must develop a sense for how and what people share.

When the privacy options available to us change, we are more likely to question the system than to alter our own behavior. But such changes strain our relationships and undermine our ability to navigate broad social norms. People who can be whoever they want, wherever they want, are a privileged minority.

How People Maintain Privacy Online

A 2013 poll showed Americans use a variety of tactics to avoid being observed online.

Percent of adult Internet users who say they have:

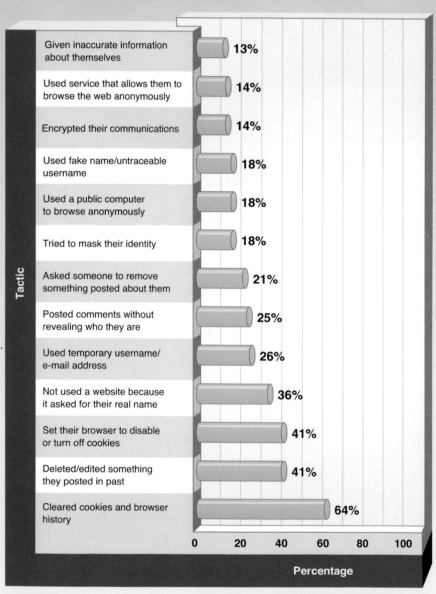

Tactic	Percentage
Given inaccurate information about themselves	13%
Used service that allows them to browse the web anonymously	14%
Encrypted their communications	14%
Used fake name/untraceable username	18%
Used a public computer to browse anonymously	18%
Tried to mask their identity	18%
Asked someone to remove something posted about them	21%
Posted comments without revealing who they are	25%
Used temporary username/e-mail address	26%
Not used a website because it asked for their real name	36%
Set their browser to disable or turn off cookies	41%
Deleted/edited something they posted in past	41%
Cleared cookies and browser history	64%

Percentage

Taken from: Pew Research Center's Internet & American Life Project Omnibus Survey, July 11–14, 2013.

As social media become more embedded in everyday society, the mismatch between the rule-based privacy that software offers and the subtler, intuitive ways that humans understand the concept will increasingly cause cultural collisions and social slips. But people will not abandon social media, nor will privacy disappear. They will simply work harder to carve out a space for privacy as they understand it and to maintain control, whether by using pseudonyms or speaking in code.

Software Must Imitate Real Life

Instead of forcing users to do that, why not make our social software support the way we naturally handle privacy? There is much to be said for allowing the sunlight of diversity to shine. But too much sunlight scorches the earth. Let's create a forest, not a desert.

EVALUATING THE AUTHOR'S ARGUMENTS:

Danah Boyd concludes her viewpoint by saying, "Too much sunlight scorches the earth. Let's create a forest, not a desert." What does she mean by this? Write one or two paragraphs on what you think she means and whether you think the analogy is effective.

Privacy Is Underrated

Daniel J. Solove

In the following viewpoint Daniel J. Solove argues that privacy is vital—even when people have nothing to hide. Privacy is too often viewed as only necessary in the extreme, he contends, such as when people do not want their nude photos or credit card numbers circulating in public. But there is a critical need to protect seemingly mundane pieces of information, too, maintains Solove. Authorities could take disparate details of a person's life—say, the fact that she recently bought a wig and Googled the word *chemotherapy*—to deduce that she is suffering from cancer, which should be a private matter. The authorities may also arrive at false conclusions about a person's activities; for example, Solove asserts that authorities could suspect a person who has checked out books about making drugs of being a drug dealer, when in reality the person could just be researching the process to write about in a novel. Solove concludes that privacy is an underrated virtue that should be protected at all costs and in all forms, even when people feel like they have nothing to hide.

> *"Even if you have nothing to hide, the government can cause you a lot of harm."*

Daniel J. Solove, "Why Privacy Matters Even if You Have Nothing to Hide," *Chronicle of Higher Education,* May 15, 2011. Reproduced with permission.

Solove is a law professor at the George Washington University in Washington, DC, and the author of *Nothing to Hide: The False Tradeoff Between Privacy and Security.*

AS YOU READ, CONSIDER THE FOLLOWING QUESTIONS:
1. What kinds of lawful activities can privacy violations inhibit, according to Solove?
2. What is aggregation and what threat does the author say it poses to privacy?
3. What is distortion and what threat does Solove say it poses to privacy?

When the government gathers or analyzes personal information, many people say they're not worried. "I've got nothing to hide," they declare. "Only if you're doing something wrong should you worry, and then you don't deserve to keep it private."

The nothing-to-hide argument pervades discussions about privacy. The data-security expert Bruce Schneier calls it the "most common retort against privacy advocates." The legal scholar Geoffrey Stone refers to it as an "all-too-common refrain." In its most compelling form, it is an argument that the privacy interest is generally minimal, thus making the contest with security concerns a foreordained victory for security. . . .

Everybody Has Something to Hide

I encountered the nothing-to-hide argument so frequently in news interviews, discussions, and the like that I decided to probe the issue. I asked the readers of my blog, *Concurring Opinions*, whether there are good responses to the nothing-to-hide argument. I received a torrent of comments:

- My response is "So do you have curtains?" or "Can I see your credit-card bills for the last year?"
- So my response to the "If you have nothing to hide . . ." argument is simply, "I don't need to justify my position. You need to justify yours. Come back with a warrant."

- I don't have anything to hide. But I don't have anything I feel like showing you, either.
- If you have nothing to hide, then you don't have a life.
- Show me yours and I'll show you mine.
- It's not about having anything to hide, it's about things not being anyone else's business.
- Bottom line, [former Soviet leader] Joe Stalin would [have] loved it. Why should anyone have to say more?

On the surface, it seems easy to dismiss the nothing-to-hide argument. Everybody probably has something to hide from somebody. As [Russian novelist] Aleksandr Solzhenitsyn declared, "Everyone is guilty of something or has something to conceal. All one has to do is look hard enough to find what it is." Likewise, in Friedrich Dürrenmatt's novella "Traps," which involves a seemingly innocent man put on trial by a group of retired lawyers in a mock-trial game, the man inquires what his crime shall be. "An altogether minor matter," replies the prosecutor. "A crime can always be found."

The Extreme Version of the Argument

One can usually think of something that even the most open person would want to hide. As a commenter to my blog post noted, "If you have nothing to hide, then that quite literally means you are willing to let me photograph you naked? And I get full rights to that photograph—so I can show it to your neighbors?" The Canadian privacy expert David Flaherty expresses a similar idea when he argues: "There is no sentient human being in the Western world who has little or no regard for his or her personal privacy; those who would attempt such claims cannot withstand even a few minutes' questioning about intimate aspects of their lives without capitulating to the intrusiveness of certain subject matters."

But such responses attack the nothing-to-hide argument only in its most extreme form, which isn't particularly strong. In a less extreme form, the nothing-to-hide argument refers not to all personal information but only to the type of data the government is likely to collect. Retorts to the nothing-to-hide argument about exposing people's naked bodies or their deepest secrets are relevant only if the government is likely to gather this kind of information. In many

Data-security expert Bruce Schneier (pictured) calls the "I have nothing to hide" argument the most common retort to privacy advocates' concerns.

instances, hardly anyone will see the information, and it won't be disclosed to the public. Thus, some might argue, the privacy interest is minimal, and the security interest in preventing terrorism is much more important. In this less extreme form, the nothing-to-hide argument is a formidable one. However, it stems from certain faulty assumptions about privacy and its value. . . .

The Essence of Privacy Is Complex

Most attempts to understand privacy do so by attempting to locate its essence—its core characteristics or the common denominator that links together the various things we classify under the rubric of "privacy." Privacy, however, is too complex a concept to be reduced to a singular essence. It is a plurality of different things that do not share any one element but nevertheless bear a resemblance to one another. For example, privacy can be invaded by the disclosure of your deepest secrets. It might also be invaded if you're watched by a peeping Tom, even if no secrets are ever revealed. With the disclosure of secrets, the harm is that your concealed information is spread to others. With the peeping Tom, the harm is that you're being watched. You'd probably find that creepy regardless of whether the peeper finds out anything sensitive or discloses any information to others. There are many other forms of invasion of privacy, such as blackmail and the improper use of your personal data. Your privacy can also be invaded if the government compiles an extensive dossier about you.

Privacy, in other words, involves so many things that it is impossible to reduce them all to one simple idea. And we need not do so.

In many cases, privacy issues never get balanced against conflicting interests, because courts, legislators, and others fail to recognize that privacy is implicated. People don't acknowledge certain problems, because those problems don't fit into a particular one-size-fits-all conception of privacy. Regardless of whether we call something a "privacy" problem, it still remains a problem, and problems shouldn't be ignored. We should pay attention to all of the different problems that spark our desire to protect privacy. . . .

Privacy Is Not Just About Hiding Bad Things

Commentators often attempt to refute the nothing-to-hide argument by pointing to things people want to hide. But the problem with the nothing-to-hide argument is the underlying assumption that privacy is about hiding bad things. By accepting this assumption, we concede far too much ground and invite an unproductive discussion about information that people would very likely want to hide. As the computer-security specialist Schneier aptly notes, the nothing-to-hide argument stems from a faulty "premise that privacy is about hiding a wrong." Surveillance, for example, can inhibit such lawful activities as free speech, free association, and other First Amendment rights essential for democracy.

The deeper problem with the nothing-to-hide argument is that it myopically views privacy as a form of secrecy. In contrast, understanding privacy as a plurality of related issues demonstrates that the disclosure of bad things is just one among many difficulties caused by government security measures. . . .

One such harm, for example, which I call aggregation, emerges from the fusion of small bits of seemingly innocuous data. When combined, the information becomes much more telling. By joining pieces of information we might not take pains to guard, the government can glean information about us that we might indeed wish to conceal. For example, suppose you bought a book about cancer. This purchase isn't very revealing on its own, for it indicates just an interest in the disease. Suppose you bought a wig. The purchase of a wig, by itself, could be for a number of reasons. But combine those two pieces of information, and now the inference can be made that you have cancer and are undergoing chemotherapy. That might be a fact you wouldn't mind sharing, but you'd certainly want to have the choice.

People Have a Right to Know What the Government Knows About Them

Another potential problem with the government's harvest of personal data is one I call exclusion. Exclusion occurs when people are prevented from having knowledge about how information about them is being used, and when they are barred from accessing and correcting errors in that data. Many government national-security measures involve maintaining a huge database of information that individuals cannot access. Indeed, because they involve national security, the very existence of these programs is often kept secret. This kind of information processing, which blocks subjects' knowledge and involvement, is a kind of due-process problem. It is a structural problem, involving the way people are treated by government institutions and creating a power imbalance between people and the government. To what extent should government officials have such a significant power over citizens? This issue isn't about what information people want to hide but about the power and the structure of government.

> **FAST FACT**
>
> Europeans may value privacy more than Americans do in that they demand stricter protections; for example, European nations ban facial-recognition technology that matches Facebook users to their pictures. In contrast, all Americans who use Facebook are automatically opted-in to that function.

A related problem involves secondary use. Secondary use is the exploitation of data obtained for one purpose for an unrelated purpose without the subject's consent. How long will personal data be stored? How will the information be used? What could it be used for in the

Americans Have a Substantial Digital Footprint

A 2013 poll found that the majority of Americans say an image of themselves is available online, while nearly a third say their home address can be readily found.

Percent of adult Internet users who say this information about themselves is available online:

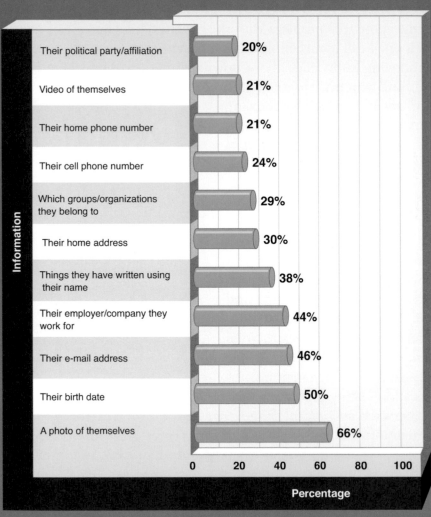

Information	Percentage
Their political party/affiliation	20%
Video of themselves	21%
Their home phone number	21%
Their cell phone number	24%
Which groups/organizations they belong to	29%
Their home address	30%
Things they have written using their name	38%
Their employer/company they work for	44%
Their e-mail address	46%
Their birth date	50%
A photo of themselves	66%

Taken from: Pew Research Center's Internet & American Life Project Omnibus Survey, July 11–14, 2013.

future? The potential uses of any piece of personal information are vast. Without limits on or accountability for how that information is used, it is hard for people to assess the dangers of the data's being in the government's control.

When Violations of Privacy Force Wrong Conclusions

Yet another problem with government gathering and use of personal data is distortion. Although personal information can reveal quite a lot about people's personalities and activities, it often fails to reflect the whole person. It can paint a distorted picture, especially since records are reductive—they often capture information in a standard-ized format with many details omitted.

For example, suppose government officials learn that a person has bought a number of books on how to manufacture methamphet-amine. That information makes them suspect that he's building a meth lab. What is missing from the records is the full story: The person is writing a novel about a character who makes meth. When he bought the books, he didn't consider how suspicious the purchase might appear to government officials, and his records didn't reveal the reason for the purchases. Should he have to worry about govern-ment scrutiny of all his purchases and actions? Should he have to be concerned that he'll wind up on a suspicious-persons list? Even if he isn't doing anything wrong, he may want to keep his records away from government officials who might make faulty inferences from them. He might not want to have to worry about how everything he does will be perceived by officials nervously monitoring for criminal activity. He might not want to have a computer flag him as suspicious because he has an unusual pattern of behavior. . . .

Privacy Usually Dies a Slow Death

Privacy is often threatened not by a single egregious act but by the slow accretion of a series of relatively minor acts. In this respect, pri-vacy problems resemble certain environmental harms, which occur over time through a series of small acts by different actors. Although society is more likely to respond to a major oil spill, gradual pollution by a multitude of actors often creates worse problems.

Privacy is rarely lost in one fell swoop. It is usually eroded over time, little bits dissolving almost imperceptibly until we finally begin to notice how much is gone. When the government starts monitoring the phone numbers people call, many may shrug their shoulders and say, "Ah, it's just numbers, that's all." Then the government might start monitoring some phone calls. "It's just a few phone calls, nothing more." The government might install more video cameras in public places. "So what? Some more cameras watching in a few more places. No big deal." The increase in cameras might lead to a more elaborate network of video surveillance. Satellite surveillance might be added to help track people's movements. The government might start analyzing people's bank records. "It's just my deposits and some of the bills I pay—no problem." The government may then start combing through credit-card records, then expand to Internet-service providers' records, health records, employment records, and more. Each step may seem incremental, but after a while, the government will be watching and knowing everything about us.

Even Those with Nothing to Hide Have a Lot to Lose

"My life's an open book," people might say. "I've got nothing to hide." But now the government has large dossiers of everyone's activities, interests, reading habits, finances, and health. What if the government leaks the information to the public? What if the government mistakenly determines that based on your pattern of activities, you're likely to engage in a criminal act? What if it denies you the right to fly? What if the government thinks your financial transactions look odd—even if you've done nothing wrong—and freezes your accounts? What if the government doesn't protect your information with adequate security, and an identity thief obtains it and uses it to defraud you? Even if you have nothing to hide, the government can cause you a lot of harm.

"But the government doesn't want to hurt me," some might argue. In many cases, that's true, but the government can also harm people inadvertently, due to errors or carelessness.

When the nothing-to-hide argument is unpacked, and its underlying assumptions examined and challenged, we can see how it shifts the debate to its terms, then draws power from its unfair advantage. The nothing-to-hide argument speaks to some problems but not to others. It represents a singular and narrow way of conceiving of privacy, and it wins by excluding consideration of the other problems often raised with government security measures. When engaged directly, the nothing-to-hide argument can ensnare, for it forces the debate to focus on its narrow understanding of privacy. But when confronted with the plurality of privacy problems implicated by government data collection and use beyond surveillance and disclosure, the nothing-to-hide argument, in the end, has nothing to say.

EVALUATING THE AUTHOR'S ARGUMENTS:

Viewpoint author Daniel J. Solove warns that even mundane details of a person's life should be kept private, lest the government misinterpret these details to arrive at a seriously wrong conclusion. He cites as an example an author who researches drug production; authorities might assume this person is a drug dealer. Consider certain details of your own life, from the medications you take, to the websites you visit, to the items you buy, to the subjects you research. Piece together some of these random details to find something you could be wrongly accused of. Does this make you think privacy is underrated? Explain.

Privacy Is Overrated

Richard A. Posner

> "There is a tendency to exaggerate the social value of privacy."

The value of privacy has been exaggerated, argues Richard A. Posner in the following viewpoint. He argues that in the age of terrorism, Americans' expectations of privacy threaten the safety of all of society. The government needs to be able to monitor public places, personal communications, and other data if it is to isolate the individuals who seek to harm everyone else. Posner sees no real loss from these efforts; privacy, he says, is largely about controlling our public image, the same way corporations seek to control the image of the products they market. In his opinion, having the ability to market ourselves is not worth a reduction in our safety. He concludes that antiterrorism efforts offer Americans much more than do privacy laws, and thus society should err on the side of safety rather than of privacy.

Posner is a judge with the US Court of Appeals for the Seventh Circuit. He is also a senior lecturer at the University of Chicago Law School.

AS YOU READ, CONSIDER THE FOLLOWING QUESTIONS:
1. What word does not appear anywhere in the Constitution, according to Posner?
2. What does the word *paternalistic* mean, as used by the author?
3. What, in the context of Posner's argument, is a two-way street?

This past Monday Mayor [Michael] Bloomberg said that in the wake of the Boston Marathon bombings, the country's interpretation of the Constitution "will have to change" in order to enable more effective prevention of and response to terrorist attacks and other violence, such as attacks on schoolchildren.

In particular, he wants a more welcoming attitude toward surveillance cameras, which played a crucial role in the apprehension of the Boston Marathon bombers—and would have been crucial had Tamerlan and Dzhokhar Tsarnaev come to New York to detonate a bomb in Times Square, as they apparently planned to. (Bloomberg has also announced a "Domain Awareness System" that will consolidate and distribute information received by the cameras and other tracking devices.)

All of which is to say that he wants concerns with privacy to take second place to concerns with security.

I strongly agree, though I'm not sure that the Constitution will have to be reinterpreted in order to enable the shift of emphasis that he (and I) favor. Neither the word "privacy" nor even the concept appears anywhere in the Constitution, and the current Supreme Court is highly sensitive, as it should be, to security needs. The Court can and doubtless will adjust the balance between privacy and security to reflect the increase in long-run threats to the lives of Americans.

There is a tendency to exaggerate the social value of privacy. I value my privacy as much as the next person, but there is a difference between what is valuable to an individual and what is valuable to society. Thirty-five years ago, when I was a law professor rather than a judge, I published an article called "The Right of Privacy," in which I pointed out that "privacy" is really just a euphemism for concealment, for hiding specific things about ourselves from others.

We conceal aspects of our person, our conduct and our history that, if known, would make it more difficult for us to achieve our personal goals. We don't want our arrest record to be made public; our medical history to be made public; our peccadilloes to be made public; and so on. We want to present sanitized versions of ourselves to the world. We market ourselves the way sellers of consumer products market their wares—highlighting the good, hiding the bad.

I do not argue that all concealment is bad. There is nothing wrong with concealing wealth in order to avoid being targeted by thieves or concealing embarrassing personal facts, such as a deformity or being related to a notorious criminal, that would not cause a rational person to shun us but might complicate our social and business relations.

There may even be justification for allowing the concealment of facts that might, but should not, cause a person to be shunned. Laws that place a person's arrest (as distinct from conviction) record behind a veil of secrecy are based on a belief that prospective employers would exaggerate the significance of such a record, not realizing, for example, that arrests are often based on mistakes by witnesses or police officers, or are for trivial infractions.

Privacy-protecting laws are paternalistic; they are based on a skepticism regarding whether people can make sensible evaluations of an arrest record or other private facts that enter the public domain.

Still, a good deal of privacy just facilitates the personal counterpart of the false advertising of goods and services, and by doing so, reduces the well-being of society as a whole.

I am not suggesting that privacy laws be repealed. I don't think that they do much harm, and they do some good, as just indicated. But I don't think they serve the public interest as well as civil libertarians contend, and so I don't think that such laws confer social benefits comparable to those of methods of surveillance that are effective against criminal and especially terrorist assaults.

More than effective: indispensable. How much more havoc might the two Boston Marathon bombers have wreaked had they remained unidentified for weeks?

> ## FAST FACT
>
> Privacy is not mentioned in the Bill of Rights or the Constitution. It was not considered a right until 1965, when the Supreme Court ruled in *Griswold v. Connecticut* that a law banning the dissemination of information on birth control infringed on married couples' privacy.

Former federal judge Richard A. Posner (pictured) says that antiterrorism efforts offer Americans much more than privacy and that society should err on the side of safety rather than privacy.

The critics of surveillance cameras invoke the specter of the telescreen, a two-way television that thus operates as a surveillance camera, which figures in George Orwell's great novel *Nineteen Eighty-Four*.

But the critics miss two important distinctions. The first is that the telescreen is inside people's homes—in every room, and monitored by state security personnel ("Big Brother is watching you"). The second distinction is that the nation in Orwell's novel—"Airstrip One" (actually England)—is a Soviet-style totalitarian dictatorship.

Americans Accept That Monitoring Public Places Can Prevent Terrorism

A CNN/*Time*/ORC poll taken just after the Boston Marathon bombing on April 15, 2013, found that although Americans are wary of giving up liberty in exchange for security, the majority recognized that security requires monitoring public areas.

Question: "Here are some increased powers of investigation that law enforcement agencies might use when dealing with people suspected of terrorist activity, which would also affect our civil liberties. Which do you favor?"

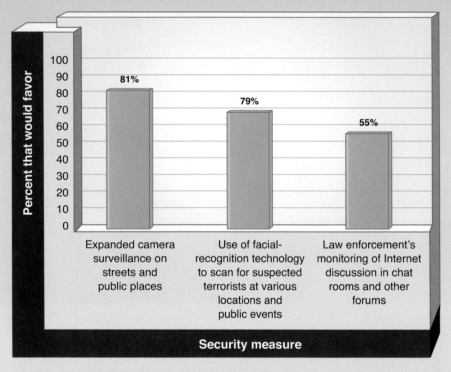

Taken from: CNN/*Time*/ORC, April 30, 2013.

(Coincidentally, England today apparently has more surveillance cameras than any other nation, some 4 million.)

Our government is not totalitarian, and surveillance cameras, when indoors (in retail stores for example), are generally invited and controlled by the owner of the premises. The surveillance cameras installed by the government are, by and large, in public areas, mainly streets, where privacy is anyway limited by the fact that one is visible and audible to other people.

True, the cameras create a record, as ordinary eavesdropping does not, but is this enough of a difference to offset the security benefits of surveillance? I think not. I live in a city—Chicago—that is said to have more than 10,000 public and private surveillance cameras. I am not troubled by them.

Critics argue that surveillance cameras don't prevent terrorism or other criminal attacks but merely facilitate apprehension of the malefactors. Obviously, surveillance cameras didn't prevent the Boston Marathon attacks. But they may well have prevented further attacks planned by the bombers, including whatever destruction they may have attempted to cause in New York City.

Moreover, the criticism ignores deterrence. By increasing the likelihood that terrorists or other criminals will be apprehended, surveillance cameras increase the expected cost of punishment. That will not deter all attacks, but it will deter many.

Civil liberties groups, notably the Electronic Frontier Foundation and the Electronic Privacy Information Center, of course do not limit their concerns to surveillance cameras. They worry, too, about governmental surveillance of people's computer files and other stored data.

But I don't think they appreciate that this is a two-way street. Surveillance technology used by our government is also used by our enemies. We must keep up; we cannot resign from the technological revolution.

EVALUATING THE AUTHOR'S ARGUMENTS:

In this viewpoint Richard A. Posner argues that privacy is not all that important for people who have nothing particularly bad to hide. In the previous viewpoint Daniel J. Solove argues that privacy is important, especially when people have nothing particularly bad to hide. After reading both viewpoints, with which author do you agree on this point? Why, and what swayed you?

Chapter 2

What Is the Relationship Between Privacy and Security?

Police monitor more than four thousand security cameras at the Lower Manhattan Security Center in New York.

Americans Should Trade Some Privacy for Increased Security

Thomas L. Friedman

"Yes, I worry about potential government abuse of privacy from a program designed to prevent another 9/11. . . . But I worry even more about another 9/11."

Thomas L. Friedman is a Pulitzer Prize–winning columnist for the *New York Times*. In this viewpoint, Friedman argues that Americans must be willing to trade at least a little privacy if they want the government to be able to protect them from terrorist attacks. He contends that giving up a little bit of privacy now—such as allowing the government to monitor certain kinds of communications, with strict oversight—helps prevent the government's needing to further invade privacy in the event of another terrorist attack. Friedman argues that current antiterrorism surveillance programs do not violate anyone's civil liberties and, in his opinion, are well-crafted programs that help prevent the kinds of attacks America has suffered in the past. Friedman maintains that if Americans want to stay safe, they must allow their government to monitor at least some level of communications, so it can find the terrorists living among us.

Thomas L. Friedman, "Blowing a Whistle," *New York Times,* June 12, 2013. Reproduced with permission.

AS YOU READ, CONSIDER THE FOLLOWING QUESTIONS:
1. What, according to Friedman, could end open society as America currently knows it?
2. What is Friedman's opinion of Edward Snowden, who leaked classified documents about the National Security Agency's surveillance program?
3. What does the author refer to by his expression "needles in haystacks"?

I'm glad I live in a country with people who are vigilant in defending civil liberties. But as I listen to the debate about the disclosure of two government programs designed to track suspected phone and e-mail contacts of terrorists, I do wonder if some of those who unequivocally defend this disclosure are behaving as if 9/11 never happened—that the *only* thing we have to fear is government intrusion in our lives, not the intrusion of those who gather in secret cells in Yemen, Afghanistan and Pakistan and plot how to topple our tallest buildings or bring down U.S. airliners with bombs planted inside underwear, tennis shoes or computer printers.

The Threat of Terrorism Is Greater than the One to Civil Liberties

Yes, I worry about potential government abuse of privacy from a program designed to prevent another 9/11—abuse that, so far, does not appear to have happened. But I worry even more about another 9/11. That is, I worry about something that's already happened once—that was staggeringly costly—and that terrorists aspire to repeat.

I worry about that even more, not because I don't care about civil liberties, but because what I cherish most about America is our open society, and I believe that if there is one more 9/11—or worse, an attack involving nuclear material—it could lead to the end of the open society as we know it. If there were another 9/11, I fear that 99 percent of Americans would tell their members of Congress: "Do whatever you need to do to, privacy be damned, just make sure this does not happen again." *That* is what I fear most.

That is why I'll reluctantly, very reluctantly, trade off the government using data mining to look for suspicious patterns in phone numbers called and e-mail addresses—and then have to go to a judge to get a warrant to actually look at the content under guidelines set by Congress—to prevent a day where, out of fear, we give government a license to look at anyone, any e-mail, any phone call, anywhere, anytime.

A Logical Anti-Terrorism Program

So I don't believe that Edward Snowden, the leaker of all this secret material is some heroic whistle-blower. No, I believe Snowden is

The author does not believe Edward Snowden (pictured), who leaked National Security Agency (NSA) surveillance activities, is a heroic whistle-blower.

someone who needed a whistleblower. He needed someone to challenge him with the argument that we don't live in a world any longer where our government can protect its citizens from real, not imagined, threats without using big data—where we still have an edge—under constant judicial review. It's not ideal. But if one more 9/11-scale attack gets through, the cost to civil liberties will be so much greater.

A hat tip to Andrew Sullivan for linking on his blog to an essay by David Simon, the creator of HBO's "The Wire." For me, it cuts right to the core of the issue.

"You would think that the government was listening in to the secrets of 200 million Americans from the reaction and the hyperbole being tossed about," wrote Simon.

And you would think that rather than a legal court order, which is an inevitable consequence of legislation that we drafted and passed, something illegal had been discovered to the government's shame. Nope. . . . The only thing new here, from a legal standpoint, is the scale on which the F.B.I. and N.S.A. are apparently attempting to cull anti-terrorism leads from that data. . . . I know it's big and scary that the government wants a database of all phone calls. And it's scary that they're paying attention to the Internet. And it's scary that your cellphones have GPS installed. . . . The question is not should the resulting data exist. It does. . . . The question is more fundamental: Is government accessing the data for the legitimate public safety needs of the society, or are they accessing it in ways that abuse individual liberties and violate personal privacy—and in a manner that is unsupervised. And to that, *The Guardian* and those who are wailing jeremiads about this pretend-discovery of U.S. big data collection are noticeably silent. We don't know of any actual abuse.

We do need to be constantly on guard for abuses. But the fact is, added Simon, that for at least the last two presidencies "this kind of data collection has been a baseline logic of an American anti-terrorism effort that is effectively asked to find the needles before they are planted into haystacks, to prevent even such modest, grass-rooted conspiracies as the Boston Marathon bombing before they occur."

Americans Want Security More than Privacy

Polls since 2006 show that Americans consistently say it is more important for the government to investigate terrorist threats, even if it means sacrificing personal privacy.

Question: "What do you think is more important right now: for the federal government to investigate possible terrorist threats, even if that intrudes on personal privacy; or for the federal government not to intrude on personal privacy, even if that limits its ability to investigate possible terrorist threats?"

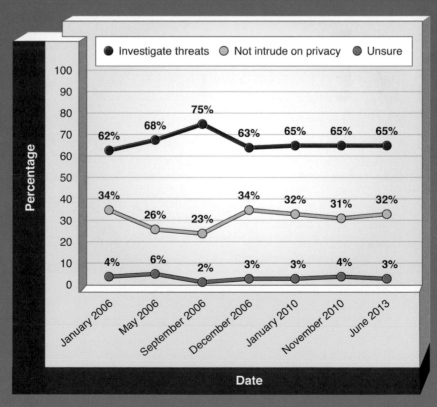

Taken from: Pew Research Center/*Washington Post* Poll, June 6–9, 2013.

Finding Needles in Haystacks Requires Reduced Privacy

To be sure, secret programs, like the virtually unregulated drone attacks, can lead to real excesses that have to be checked. But here is what is also real, Simon concluded:

> Those planes really did hit those buildings. And that bomb did indeed blow up at the finish line of the Boston Marathon. And we really are in a continuing, low-intensity, high-risk conflict with a diffuse, committed and ideologically motivated enemy. And, for a moment, just imagine how much bloviating would be wafting across our political spectrum if, in the wake of an incident of domestic terrorism, an American president and his administration had failed to take full advantage of the existing telephonic data to do what is possible to find those needles in the haystacks.

And, I'd add, not just bloviating. Imagine how many real restrictions to our beautiful open society we would tolerate if there were another attack on the scale of 9/11. Pardon me if I blow that whistle.

EVALUATING THE AUTHOR'S ARGUMENTS:

Viewpoint author Thomas L. Friedman hinges his argument on the idea that terrorists pose a significant threat to Americans. How would Conor Friedersdorf, author of the following viewpoint, respond to this claim? Write two or three sentences on how you think Friedersdorf would respond. Then, state with which author you agree and why, noting how serious you think the threat from terrorism is and how much privacy you are willing to sacrifice to stay safe from attack.

Americans Should Not Trade Much Privacy for Increased Security

Conor Friedersdorf

"It is not rational to give up massive amounts of privacy and liberty to stay marginally safer from a threat that . . . endangers the average American far less than his or her daily commute."

In the following viewpoint Conor Friedersdorf argues that it is irrational for Americans to allow the government to invade their privacy under the pretense of protecting them from terrorist attacks. He agrees it is very scary to imagine being killed in a terrorist attack. But the fear of dying in such an attack is far greater than the actual risk—Americans are far more likely to die in traffic accidents, from diabetes, and from gun accidents. Friedersdorf says that Americans would never tolerate invasions to their privacy to stop deaths caused by drunk driving accidents or medical tragedies, so it makes no sense for them to tolerate privacy invasions to combat terrorism, which statistically poses a far lesser threat. Friedersdorf urges Americans to recognize that giving up their privacy to supposedly combat terrorism does not make sense given the minuscule risk of dying in such an attack.

Friedersdorf is a staff writer for the *Atlantic*, a monthly magazine.

AS YOU READ, CONSIDER THE FOLLOWING QUESTIONS:
1. How many Americans does Friedersdorf say died from diabetes in 2001?
2. How many Americans does Friedersdorf say were killed in drunk-driving accidents between 1999 and 2010?
3. In 2011 how many Americans does the author say died in terrorist attacks, and how does this compare to the number who died in traffic accidents?

The image is still powerful, isn't it?

So are the anger, and the memories.

Most Americans don't just remember where they were on September 11, 2001—they remember feeling frightened. Along with anger, that's one emotion I felt, despite watching the attacks from a different continent. That week, you couldn't have paid me to get on a plane to New York or Washington, D.C. Even today, I'm aware that terrorists target exactly the sorts of places that I frequent. I fly a lot, sometimes out of LAX [Los Angeles International Airport]. I've ridden the subway systems in London [England] and Madrid [Spain]. I visit Washington and New York several times a year. I live in Greater Los Angeles. [All of these have been terrorist targets.]

But like most people, I've never let fear of terrorism stop me from enjoying life's opportunities and pleasures. I wouldn't have my current job if I hadn't moved to New York for graduate school in 2005, and then to Washington a couple of years later. It isn't that I never thought, or worried, about the fact that those cities are prime targets of terrorism. Rather, my intellect got the better of my fears, something that happens every time I get on a commercial airliner and remind myself that it's far safer than making the same trip by car; or every time that I jump into the Pacific Ocean, knowing that, as terrifying as sharks are, it's unlikely I'll be killed by one.

Terrorism Kills Relatively Few People

As individuals, Americans are generally good at denying [terrorist network] al-Qaeda the pleasure of terrorizing us into submission. Our cities are bustling; our subways are packed every rush hour; there doesn't seem to be an empty seat on any flight I'm ever on. But as a collective, irrational cowardice is getting the better of our polity. Terrorism isn't something we're ceding liberty to fight because the threat is especially dire compared to other dangers of the modern world. All sorts of things kill us in far greater numbers. Rather, like airplane crashes and shark attacks, acts of terror are scarier than most causes of death. The seeming contradictions in how we treat different threats suggest that we aren't trading civil liberties for security, but a *sense* of security. We aren't empowering the national-security state so that we're safer, but so we *feel* safer.

Of course we should dedicate significant resources and effort to stopping terrorism. But consider some hard facts. In 2001, the year when America suffered an unprecedented terrorist attack—by far the biggest in its history—roughly 3,000 people died from terrorism in the U.S.

Let's put that in context. That same year in the United States:

> ## FAST FACT
>
> Then National Security Agency (NSA) deputy director John C. Inglis testified in July 2013 that the agency could not identify a single case in which its secret collection of millions of Americans' phone records helped prevent a terrorist attack.

- 71,372 died of diabetes.
- 29,573 were killed by guns.
- 13,290 were killed in drunk driving accidents.

That's what things looked like *at the all-time peak for deaths by terrorism.* Now let's take a longer view. We'll choose an interval that still includes the biggest terrorist attack in American history: 1999 to 2010.

Again, terrorists killed roughly 3,000 people in the United States. And in that interval, roughly 360,000 were killed by guns (actually, the figure the CDC [Centers for Disease Control and Prevention] gives is 364,483—in other words, by rounding, I just elided [omitted] more

The author points out that roughly 150,000 Americans have died in drunk-driving accidents since the 9/11 attacks, more than fifty times the number of Americans killed in terrorist attacks; thus, it seems unreasonable to trade privacy for security against such attacks.

gun deaths than there were total terrorism deaths). Roughly 150,000 were killed in drunk-driving accidents.

Measured in lives lost, *during an interval that includes the biggest terrorist attack in American history,* guns posed a threat to American lives that was *more than 100 times greater* than the threat of terrorism. Over the same interval, drunk driving threatened our safety *50 times more than terrorism.*

Those aren't the only threats many times more deadly than terrorism, either.

It Is Irrational to Cede Liberty for Security

The CDC estimates that food poisoning kills roughly 3,000 Americans every year. Every year, food-borne illness takes as many lives in the U.S. as were lost during the high outlier of terrorism deaths. It's a killer more deadly than terrorism. Should we cede a significant amount of liberty to fight it?

Government officials, much of the media, and most American citizens talk about terrorism as if they're totally oblivious to this context—as if it is different than all other threats we face, in both kind and degree. Since *The Guardian* and other news outlets started revealing the scope of the surveillance state last week [in June 2013], numerous commentators and government officials, including President [Barack] Obama himself, have talked about the need to properly "balance" liberty and security.

The U.S. should certainly try to prevent terrorist attacks, and there is a lot that government can and has done since 9/11 to improve security in ways that are totally unobjectionable. But it is not rational to give up massive amounts of privacy and liberty to stay marginally safer from a threat that, however scary, endangers the average American *far less* than his or her daily commute. In 2011, 32,367 Americans died in traffic fatalities. Terrorism killed 17 U.S. civilians that year. How many Americans feared dying in their vehicles more than dying in a terrorist attack?

Certainly not me! I irrationally find terrorism far scarier than the sober incompetents and irresponsible drunks who surround my vehicle every time I take a carefree trip down a Los Angeles freeway. The idea that the government could keep me safe from terrorism is very emotionally appealing.

But intellectually, I know two things:

1. America has preserved liberty and privacy in the face of threats far greater than terrorism has so far posed (based on the number of people actually killed in terrorist attacks), and we've been better off for it.
2. Ceding liberty and privacy to keep myself safe from terrorism doesn't even guarantee that I'll be safer! It's possible that the surveillance state will prove invasive and ineffective. Or that giving the state so much latitude to exercise extreme power in secret will itself threaten my safety.

We Must Not React Emotionally to Terrorism

I understand, as well as anyone, that terrorism is scary. But it's time to stop reacting to it with our guts, and to start reacting with our brains, not just when we're deciding to vacation in Washington or New York, but also when we're making policy together as free

Comparing Gun and Terrorism Deaths in the United States, 1999 to 2010

Deaths from terrorism account for a tiny percentage of all deaths, and pale in comparison to deaths from other sources, like guns.

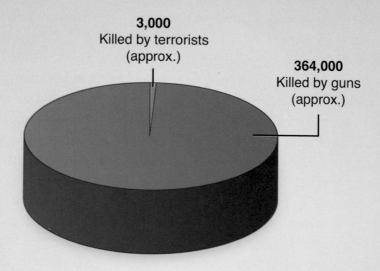

3,000
Killed by terrorists
(approx.)

364,000
Killed by guns
(approx.)

Taken from: Conor Friedersdorf. "The Irrationality of Giving Up This Much Liberty to Fight Terror." *Atlantic*, June 10, 2013.

citizens. Civil libertarians are not demanding foolish or unreasonable courage when they suggest that the threat of terrorism isn't so great as to warrant massive spying on innocent Americans and the creation of a permanent database that practically guarantees eventual abuse.

Americans would never welcome a secret surveillance state to reduce diabetes deaths, or gun deaths, or drunk-driving deaths by 3,000 per year. Indeed, Congress regularly votes down far less invasive policies meant to address those problems because they offend our notions of liberty. So what sense does it make to suggest, as Obama does, that "balancing" liberty with safety from terrorism—which kills *far fewer* than 3,000 Americans annually—compels those same invasive methods to be granted, in secret, as long as terrorists are plotting?

That only makes sense if the policy is aimed at lessening not just wrongful deaths, but also exaggerated fears and emotions. Hence my refusal to go along. Do you know what scares me more than terrorism? A polity that reacts to fear by ceding more autonomy and power to its secret police.

EVALUATING THE AUTHOR'S ARGUMENTS:

In this viewpoint Conor Friedersdorf says that Americans would never tolerate giving up privacy to combat threats such as drunk driving or diabetes, and since terrorism poses far less of a risk to one's life and safety, they should not tolerate giving up privacy to combat terrorism, either. What do you think of his reasoning? In your opinion, does terrorism pose the same kind of threat as diabetes, guns, or driving? What are the similarities? What are the differences? After considering his argument, state whether you agree with him, and why.

Government's Metadata Program Is Sound

"This nation has real problems if its people, at least here, can't trust the combined actions of the executive branch and the Congress, backstopped by federal judges sworn to protect our individual liberties."

Roger Pilon and Richard A. Epstein

The government program that collects citizen metadata (data about data) is reasonable, sound, and effective, argues Roger Pilon and Richard A. Epstein in the following viewpoint. They discuss a program by the National Security Agency that monitors the numbers, times, and patterns of phone calls and other communications but *not* their content. Pilon and Epstein say this is within the confines of the law—under the Constitution, metadata collection constitutes a reasonable search, and the fact that all three branches of government have approved of the program is a ringing endorsement of its legality. In the authors' opinion, allowing the government to access this data is a smart, sensible way to prevent terrorist attacks, one that poses very little threat to Americans' privacy. They conclude the government can be trusted to not use

Roger Pilon and Richard A. Epstein, "Government's Metadata Program Is Sound," *Chicago Tribune,* June 12, 2013. Reproduced with permission.

the information they collect for any other purpose than to keep Americans safe.

Pilon is vice president for legal affairs at the Cato Institute, a Washington, DC–based libertarian think tank, and director of Cato's Center for Constitutional Studies. Epstein is a law professor at New York University Law School.

AS YOU READ, CONSIDER THE FOLLOWING QUESTIONS:
1. What do the authors say is prevented by the Fourth Amendment?
2. What was at issue in the Supreme Court case *Smith v. Maryland*, according to Pilon and Epstein?
3. Who is Najibullah Zazi, as described by the authors?

President Barack Obama is under harsh attack for stating the obvious: No amount of government ingenuity will guarantee the American people 100 percent security, 100 percent privacy and zero inconvenience. He was answering a burst of more heated responses from left and right alike to the "news" that for years the National Security Agency has been collecting metadata about Americans' phone calls and certain foreign Internet communications.

Legally, the president is on secure footing under the Patriot Act, which Congress passed shortly after 9/11 and has since reauthorized by large bipartisan majorities. As he stressed, the program has enjoyed the continued support of all three branches of the federal government. It has been free of political abuse since its inception. And as he rightly added, this nation has real problems if its people, at least here, can't trust the combined actions of the executive branch and the Congress, backstopped by federal judges sworn to protect our individual liberties secured by the Bill of Rights.

In asking for our trust, Obama would be on stronger ground, of course, if the NSA controversy had not followed hard on the heels of the ongoing Benghazi, IRS and AP/Fox News scandals—to say nothing of Attorney General Eric Holder's problems. But give Obama due credit: We can recall no other instance in which he announced

Who Users Avoid Online

A 2013 poll found that 55 percent of Internet users have taken steps to hide from specific people or organizations online. However, most fear intrusion from hackers, criminals, advertisers, and people they know—just 5 percent said they hide from the government.

Percent of adult Internet users who say they have used the Internet in ways to avoid being observed or seen by . . .

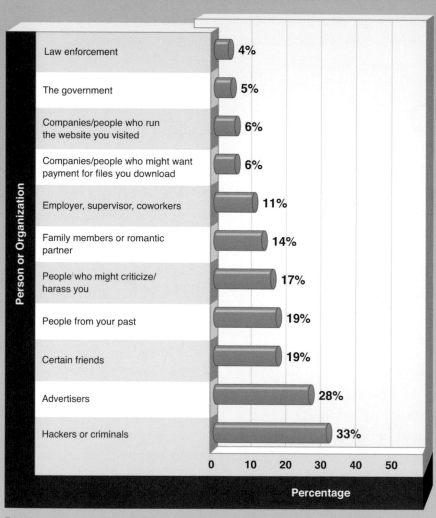

Person or Organization	Percentage
Law enforcement	4%
The government	5%
Companies/people who run the website you visited	6%
Companies/people who might want payment for files you download	6%
Employer, supervisor, coworkers	11%
Family members or romantic partner	14%
People who might criticize/harass you	17%
People from your past	19%
Certain friends	19%
Advertisers	28%
Hackers or criminals	33%

Taken from: Pew Research Center's Internet & American Life Project Omnibus Survey, July 11–14, 2013.

publicly that the responsibilities of his office have changed his mind. And for the better—here's why.

In domestic and foreign affairs, the basic function of government is to protect our liberty, without unnecessarily violating that liberty in the process. The text of the Fourth Amendment grasps that essential trade-off by allowing searches, but not "unreasonable" ones. That instructive, albeit vague, accommodation has led courts to craft legal rules that, first, define what a search is and, second, indicate the circumstances under which one is justified. In the realm of foreign intelligence gathering, recognizing the need for secrecy and their own limitations, judges have shown an acute awareness of the strength of the public interest in national security. They have rightly deferred to Congress and the executive branch, allowing executive agencies to engage in the limited surveillance that lies at the opposite pole from ransacking a single person's sensitive papers for political purposes.

That deference is especially appropriate now that Congress, through the Patriot Act, has set a delicate balance that enables the executive branch to carry out its basic duty to protect us from another 9/11 while respecting our privacy as much as possible. Obviously, reasonable people can

have reasonable differences over how that balance is struck. But on this question, political deliberation has done its job, because everyone on both sides of the aisle is seeking the right constitutional balance.

In 1979, in *Smith v. Maryland*, the U.S. Supreme Court addressed that balance when it held that using a pen register to track telephone numbers did not count as an invasion of privacy, even in ordinary criminal cases. That's just what the government is doing here on a grand scale. The metadata it examines in its effort to uncover suspicious patterns enables it to learn the numbers called, the locations of the parties, and the lengths of the calls. The government does not know—as some have charged—whether you've called your psychiatrist, lawyer

Najibullah Zazi's (pictured) 2009 New York subway bombing plot was uncovered by the National Security Agency's PRISM Internet spying program by intercepting key e-mails.

or lover. The names linked to the phone numbers are not available to the government before a court grants a warrant on proof of probable cause, just as the Fourth Amendment requires. Indeed, once that warrant is granted to examine content, the content can be used only for national security issues, not even ordinary police work.

As the president said, the process involves some necessary loss of privacy. But it's trivial, certainly in comparison to the losses that would have arisen if the government had failed to discern the pattern that let it thwart the 2009 New York subway bombing plot by Colorado airport shuttle driver Najibullah Zazi, an Afghan-American, who was prosecuted and ultimately pleaded guilty.

The critics miss the forest for the trees. Yes, government officials might conceivably misuse some of the trillions of bits of metadata they examine using sophisticated algorithms. But one abuse is no pattern of abuses. And even one abuse is not likely to happen given the safeguards in place. The cumulative weight of the evidence attests to the soundness of the program. The critics would be more credible if they could identify a pattern of government abuses. But after 12 years of continuous practice, they can't cite even a single case. We should be thankful that here, at least, government has done its job and done it well.

EVALUATING THE AUTHOR'S ARGUMENTS:

In this viewpoint Roger Pilon and Richard A. Epstein argue that the government can be trusted with citizens' metadata because such data does not reveal the content of communications, only impersonal details about its nature. How would Jay Stanley and Ben Wizner, authors of the following viewpoint, directly respond to this claim? Write two or three sentences on how you think they would respond. Then, state your opinion on the matter—is metadata collection harmless, from a privacy perspective? Why or why not?

The Government Cannot Be Trusted with Communication Metadata

Jay Stanley and Ben Wizner

> *"Metadata can be used to construct nuanced portraits of our social relationships and interactions."*

Metadata contains troves of personal information with which the government should not be trusted, argue Jay Stanley and Ben Wizner in the following viewpoint. Stanley and Wizner explain that a lot of people think metadata is harmless because it does not contain the content of communications, only details such as a phone call's location or its length of time. But much can be gleaned about a person from knowing just this basic information, argue the authors. They claim it is possible to determine whether a person has a substance abuse, gambling, or health problem; whether they have been unfaithful to their spouse; what their sexual orientation is; and other deeply personal pieces of information. They say the government should not be trusted with such sensitive information about citizens who have done nothing wrong. They conclude that metadata does contain potentially sensitive information, and privacy laws need to be updated to reflect the nature of digital communications.

Wizner is the director and Stanley is a senior policy analyst with the American Civil Liberties Union's Speech, Privacy, and Technology Project, which is dedicated to protecting and expanding the First Amendment's right to privacy.

AS YOU READ, CONSIDER THE FOLLOWING QUESTIONS:
1. Who is David Petraeus, as described by the authors?
2. According to Stanley and Wizner, how could the government ascertain whether someone has a drinking problem simply by looking at their metadata?
3. What, according to the authors, was the Supreme Court's decision in *Smith v. Maryland*?

I n the wake of [the British newspaper] *The Guardian*'s remarkable revelation [in June 2013] that the National Security Agency [NSA] is collecting phone records from millions of Americans, defenders of this dragnet surveillance program are insisting that the intelligence agency isn't eavesdropping on the calls—it's just scooping up "metadata." The implication is that civil liberties complaints about Orwellian[1] surveillance tactics are overblown.

Metadata Can Reveal Our Intimate Secrets

But any suggestion that Americans have nothing to worry about from this dragnet collection of communications metadata is wrong. Even without intercepting the content of communications, the government can use metadata to learn our most intimate secrets—anything from whether we have a drinking problem to whether we're gay or straight. The suggestion that metadata is "no big deal"—a view that, regrettably, is still reflected in the law—is entirely out of step with the reality of modern communications.

1. George Orwell was a political journalist and author of the dystopian novel *1984*, about a future totalitarian surveillance state.

So what exactly is metadata? Simply, if the "data" of a communication is the content of an email or phone call, this is data *about* the data—the identities of the sender and recipient, and the time, date, duration and location of a communication. This information can be extraordinarily sensitive. A Massachusetts Institute of Technology study a few years back found that reviewing people's social networking contacts alone was sufficient to determine their sexual orientation. Consider, metadata from email communications was sufficient to identify the mistress of then-CIA Director David Petraeus and then drive him out of office.

The Details Are in the Data

The "who," "when" and "how frequently" of communications are often more revealing than what is said or written. Calls between a reporter and a government whistleblower, for example, may reveal a relationship that can be incriminating all on its own.

Repeated calls to Alcoholics Anonymous, hotlines for gay teens, abortion clinics or a gambling bookie may tell you all you need to know about a person's problems. If a politician were revealed to have repeatedly called a phone sex hotline after 2:00 AM, no one would need to know what was said on the call before drawing conclusions. In addition sophisticated data-mining technologies have compounded the privacy implications by allowing the government to analyze terabytes of metadata and reveal far more details about a person's life than ever before.

Metadata Has Value Precisely Because It Contains Private Information

As technology advances, the distinction between data and metadata can be hard to distinguish. If a Website's content is data, is the Website's address metadata? The government has argued it is.

The National Security Agency's Bluffdale, Utah, metadata gathering center is where records of Americans' phone calls and e-mails are stored.

But like the list of books we check out of a library, the sites we "visit" online are really a list of things we've read. Not only do URLs often contain content—such as search terms embedded within them—but the very fact that we've visited a page with a URL such as "www. webmd.com/depression" can be every bit as revealing as the content of an email message.

For this reason, law enforcement and intelligence agencies have long appreciated the value of metadata, and the outdated view that metadata surveillance is far less invasive than eavesdropping has allowed those agencies to use powerful surveillance tools with relatively little judicial oversight.

They can do this because, decades ago, long before the Internet altered all aspects of modern communication, the Supreme Court ruled [in *Smith v. Maryland*] that when we voluntarily divulge personal information to any third party, we waive our privacy rights and lose all Fourth Amendment protection over that information.

That decision would make sense if it was about, for example, why we can't reasonably expect something to remain private when we loudly boast about it in a bar. But the court extended that logic to phone calls. The argument was that since we "share" the phone numbers we dial with the phone company—which needs that information to connect the call—we can't claim any constitutional protection when the government asks for that data.

Letting the Government Dig Through Our Digital Lives

After the Supreme Court took this wrong turn in the 1970s, Congress compounded [it] in the 1980s by codifying a lesser standard of protection for metadata. But neither the court nor Congress could have foreseen that NSA supercomputers would one day be able to mine that metadata to construct comprehensive pictures of our lives.

So we shouldn't be comforted when government officials reassure us that they're not listening to our communications—they're merely harvesting and mining our metadata. In a digital world, metadata can be used to construct nuanced portraits of our social relationships and interactions.

It's long past time for Congress to update our surveillance and privacy laws to ensure that before the government can go digging through our digital lives, it needs to demonstrate to a judge that it has good reason to believe we've done something wrong.

EVALUATING THE AUTHOR'S ARGUMENTS:

In this viewpoint Jay Stanley and Ben Wizner use facts, examples, and reasoning to make their argument that the government should not be trusted with citizens' metadata. They do not, however, use any quotations to support their point. If you were to rewrite this article and insert quotations, what authorities might you quote from? Where would you place the quotations, and why?

Chapter 3

What Is the Relationship Between Privacy and Technology?

Facebook's servers are located in the company's Prineville, Oregon, data center. The fact that the National Security Agency has snooped on digital communications stored by nine Internet services, including Facebook, illustrates how aggressively personal data is being collected and analyzed by the government.

Viewpoint

1

We Should Not Sacrifice Privacy for Technological Convenience

"[Privacy is] worth cherishing and preserving in [its] own right even if it means that the much-anticipated future will take somewhat more effort and energy to construct."

Evgeny Morozov

Technological convenience is not worth giving up privacy, argues Evgeny Morozov in the following viewpoint. He discusses how Google has developed a multitude of complementary products that help users drive to unfamiliar locations, keep their appointments, organize their social networking activity, and even record what they see and with whom they interact. Morozov admits these advances are convenient and cool but warns they also require that people completely relinquish their privacy and share very personal information with a company that profits from that knowledge. Morozov contends that this is not a fair trade—our privacy is too high a price to pay for the technological revolution, because once privacy is lost it is very difficult to get back. Morozov maintains that Americans should guard their privacy, even if that means forgoing aspects of a cutting-edge technological future.

Evgeny Morozov, "Google Revolution Isn't Worth Our Privacy," *Financial Times,* August 5, 2013. Reproduced with permission.

Morozov is the author of the book *To Save Everything, Click Here: The Folly of Technological Solutionism.*

AS YOU READ, CONSIDER THE FOLLOWING QUESTIONS:
1. Who is Larry Page, as mentioned by the author?
2. What, according to Morozov, is the Grand Implant Agenda?
3. What threat does Google Now pose to privacy, in the author's opinion?

L et's give credit where it is due: Google is not hiding its revolutionary ambitions. As its co-founder Larry Page put it in 2004, eventually its search function "will be included in people's brains" so that "when you think about something and don't really know much about it, you will automatically get information".

Science fiction? The implant is a rhetorical flourish but Mr Page's utopian project is not a distant dream. In reality, the implant does not have to be connected to our brains. We carry it in our pockets—it's called a smartphone.

The Future Is Here, and It Is Invasive

So long as Google can interpret—and predict—our intentions, Mr Page's vision of a continuous and frictionless information supply could be fulfilled. However, to realise this vision, Google needs a wealth of data about us. Knowing what we search for helps—but so does knowing about our movements, our surroundings, our daily routines and our favourite cat videos.

Some of this information has been collected through our browsers but in a messy, disaggregated form. Back in 1996, Google didn't set out with a strategy for world domination. Its acquisition of services such as YouTube was driven by tactics more than strategy. While it was collecting a lot of data from its many services, from email to calendar, such data were kept in separate databases—which made the implant scenario hard to accomplish.

Thus, when last year [2012] Google announced its privacy policy, which would bring the data collected through its more than 60 online services under one roof, the move made business sense. The obvious reason for doing so is to make individual user profiles even more appealing to advertisers: when Google tracks you it can predict what ads to serve you much better than when it tracks you only across one such service.

But there is another reason, of course—and it has to do with the Grand Implant Agenda: the more Google knows about us, the easier it can make predictions about what we want—or will want in the near future. Google Now, the company's latest offering, is meant to do just that: by tracking our every email, appointment and social networking activity, it can predict where we need to be, when, and with whom. Perhaps, it might even order a car to drive us there—the whole point is to relieve us of active decision-making. The implant future is already here—it's just not evenly resisted.

Privacy Is a Fundamental Human Value

This week [April 2013], data protection authorities from six European countries showed some such resistance when they announced an effort to investigate if Google's policy violates their national privacy laws. This announcement follows several months of consultation—preceded by a letter that EU [European Union] data regulators sent to Mr Page in October—which yielded little response from Google. The letter urged the company to disclose how it processes personal data in each service and to clarify why and how it combines data that come from its multiple services.

Google believes it has met all the formal requirements on announcing the policy back in 2012. Under the current legal regime, Google, even if fined, doesn't stand to lose much from these investigations. However, if the recent proposal to create a new single EU data regulator that can fine companies up to 2 per cent of their global turnover goes through, it might present Google with a bill as high as $1bn [a billion dollars], if any breaches were found. Even if their investigations fail, European regulators must be applauded for embarking on a mission that their colleagues across the Atlantic wouldn't even dare contemplate.

Europe, with its unflinching defence of privacy as a fundamental human value, cannot afford to act disjointedly—not at a time when the most powerful company in Silicon Valley [California, home of many high-tech companies] is amassing a fleet of self-driving cars and releasing Google Glass, a line of smart glasses that some privacy advocates rightfully compare to stylish CCTV [closed-circuit TV] cameras that, for reasons unknown, we have accepted to wear on our heads.

An Intrusion into the Physical World

Google's intrusion into the physical world means that, were its privacy policy to stay in place and cover self-driving cars and Google Glass, our Internet searches might be linked to our driving routes, while our favourite cat videos might be linked to the actual cats we see in the streets. It also means that everything that Google already knows about us based on our search, email and calendar would enable it to serve us ads linked to the actual physical products and establishments we encounter via Google Glass.

For many this may be a very enticing future. We can have it, but we must also find a way to know—in great detail, not just in summary form—what happens to our data once we share it with Google, and to retain some control over what it can track and for how long.

It would also help if one could drive through the neighbourhood in one of Google's autonomous vehicles without having to log into Google Plus, the company's social network, or any other Google service.

The European regulators are not planning to thwart Google's agenda or nip innovation in the bud. This is an unflattering portrayal that might benefit Google's lobbying efforts but has no bearing in reality. Quite the opposite: it is only by taking full stock of the revolutionary nature of Google's agenda that we can get the company to act more responsibly towards its users.

> **FAST FACT**
>
> In Europe, Google must notify citizens before photographing their neighborhoods, houses, and cars for its Street View mapping program, which does not seem to affect the maps' usefulness or accuracy. Google is not required to do this in the United States.

We Must Say No

Engineering, as the tech historian Ken Alder once put it, "operates on a simple, but radical assumption: that the present is nothing more than the raw material from which to construct a better future". This might well be the case but not all raw materials are alike; if European history teaches us anything, it's that some raw materials—and privacy is certainly among them—are worth cherishing and preserving in their own right, even if it means that the much-anticipated future will take somewhat more effort and energy to construct. A revolutionary future built on shaky foundations: to that, we must say a resounding No.

EVALUATING THE AUTHOR'S ARGUMENTS:

Evgeny Morozov quotes from several sources to support the points he makes in his viewpoint. Make a list of everyone he quotes, including their credentials and the nature of their comments. Then, analyze his sources—are they credible? Are they well qualified to speak on this subject? What specific points do they support? How do they add to his argument?

A Case Against Online Privacy

Manan Kakkar

"Here's what happens if Facebook, Amazon, Bing, Google study user behavior: . . . The computer finally does what it's supposed to—start helping you in everyday life."

In the following viewpoint Manan Kakkar argues that sacrificing privacy helps companies develop more intelligent technology that is vastly more useful to people. He asserts that social media and smart technology that tracks people's whereabouts, records their preferences, and gets to know their habits, routines, and social circles enables such products to work better, return more personalized results, and help users get what they need more quickly. When services know people's likes, dislikes, whereabouts, habits, and other information, they can offer them a better experience, which Kakkar contends is what people have wanted from technology for decades. Kakkar argues that if people have a problem sacrificing their privacy, they should not use products that require them to share personal information.

Kakkar is a telecommunications engineer. His articles have appeared on technology sites such as ZDNet.com.

AS YOU READ, CONSIDER THE FOLLOWING QUESTIONS:
1. What is Amazon Silk, as described by the author?
2. What problem does Kakkar have with the suggestion that Facebook charge users monthly fees?
3. For what two reasons do companies like Facebook and Amazon track people, according to Kakkar?

The world went crazy with privacy concerns last month over news about Facebook tracking users even after they logged out was made. (It has to do with cookies.) Oh how the private lives were being spied on by Mark Zuckerberg caved in a bunker with the rest of the Facebook employees monitoring and tracking every Facebook user much like Lucius Fox and Batman; only to sell this data to scamming advertisers and pesky telemarketers who want to sell every married guy a pair of lingerie for he searched about *what women like* or the telemarketer from Bangladesh who will keep calling you to buy a plastic *squeeze to fart* cow since you played Farmville. Oh how dare you, Zuckerberg?!

Then Jeff Bezos unveiled Amazon Silk—the browser that will predict your next click based on what other users clicked. I knew that Bezos had evil plans with that Amazon Kindle. He even looks like Lex Luthor, I knew it! He was up to no good. Privacy Jeff! Privacy! I don't want you to know that I will click on the *nude Lindsay Lohan* link after reading about her recent kerfuffle on TMZ's website. RESPECT MY PRIVACY AMAZON!

Of course all this privacy noise comes with no explanation as to what's wrong if Amazon tries to study what their users are doing on

> **FAST FACT**
>
> Many people link their cell phone to other accounts for convenience, even though doing so potentially compromises their privacy. A 2011 survey by Confident Technologies showed that 50 percent of Americans use banking or financial apps on their phones or tablets; 35 percent have online shopping apps; 77 percent use social networking on their mobile device; and 97 percent have e-mail on their phone.

the Internet. Here's what happens if Facebook, Amazon, Bing, Google study user behavior:

- Tailored search results
- Better browsing experience

The computer finally does what it's supposed to—start helping you in everyday life. Then there is the advertiser argument. If I read about

In 2011 Amazon's CEO Jeff Bezos (pictured) unveiled Amazon Silk—the browser that will predict your next click based on what other users have clicked.

men's fashion on Facebook, the ads lead me to some great websites like PRIVE or Gilt. They show me stuff that I might buy instead of emoticons to download. I've found and bought stuff through Facebook's tailored ads. Another argument is Facebook making money through my data. "O. M. G. Zucky, u r rUDe!"

So essentially, these guys want Facebook to keep offering uninterrupted cloud storage and a medium to communicate for free and not make any money to maintain/run the service. Fair enough. Dumb people exist. Let's put this in perspective: Facebook collects user data to study user behavior then shares this data with advertisers who then show you results that might be relevant and useful to you. For argument's sake this unethical and Facebook says we'll start charging users monthly subscription fees. This model will fail since there is an entry barrier and less users will be willing to use the service. This destroys the whole social aspect of Facebook since less of my friends and their friends will be on Facebook—everybody loses.

I understand privacy concerns but what I can't rationalize is what is wrong with Facebook or Amazon tracking me. They're doing so to:

- make money
- (as a side effect) provide me some value

Compared to ISPs who know everything I do, store this data for 7 years and willingly share this data with cops or cap my Internet speeds if I download too much? Let's see:

- service that knows what I do and provides me a better experience
- service that won't tell me I'm being tracked, shares this data with the cops and provides me NO benefit

I wonder who's more dangerous. From all the social media privacy rhetoric, it's clear that an opt-in service or an opt-out option makes people more comfortable about sharing information which isn't private in the first place. But the power of suggestion and perception is strong. Also, please cut the crap with all the privacy BS since clearly there is no downside unless citizens of India, Iran, North Korea, Pakistan keep feeding American servers through networks like

Facebook/Twitter only so that this data can be used by the CIA to study the country and fly unmanned drones to attack.

Taking a cue from *The Matrix*, I'll put it this way. If you're on the Internet—there is no privacy.

EVALUATING THE AUTHOR'S ARGUMENTS:

Viewpoint author Manan Kakkar hinges his argument on the idea that sacrificing privacy helps technology to better help people. What do you think? Is sacrificing privacy the only way for such technologies to prove themselves useful? Is there, or should there be, a way that technology can help people without violating their privacy?

Companies Use Technological Data Gathering Intrusively

Richard Franklin

"New technologies . . . give businesses— and governments— powerful tools to become increasingly intrusive."

Richard Franklin is a professor of business administration at the University of Pittsburgh. In the following viewpoint he argues that companies should not be trusted with people's private information. He asserts that the ways in which companies collect information about their users have become incredibly sophisticated—companies can make very accurate predictions about people's personal preferences, sexual orientation, race, shopping habits, and other characteristics, essentially enabling corporations to create a personal profile on each Internet user. They then sell this information to other companies, who can target users with precise advertisements. This system has turned Internet users into products themselves, contends Franklin. He urges people to become aware of how they are being exploited by corporations and to guard what they share about themselves online. Follow Professor Franklin on Twitter: @ProfRFranklin.

AS YOU READ, CONSIDER THE FOLLOWING QUESTIONS:
1. What is Big Data, as described by the author?
2. What are predictive analytics, as described by Franklin?
3. What percentage of the time were researchers accurately able to distinguish online between Democrats and Republicans? How often between white and black people?

You have considerable reason to be worried about your privacy these days. Countless criminals would like to steal your identity, empty your bank accounts and plunder your credit cards. You are wise to safeguard your personal information, protect yourself against phishing and avoid questionable websites.

But your privacy is also threatened—quite legally—by tech companies such as Google, Amazon, Apple, Facebook and credit-rating bureaus like Experian, Equifax and TransUnion.

Powerful Information-Collecting Tools

In the United States, there are few uniform laws or regulations regarding what these firms can collect or do with the data they collect. Meanwhile, two new technologies, Big Data and predictive analytics, give businesses—and governments—powerful tools to become increasingly intrusive.

Big Data refers to data sets so large and complex that they cannot be processed using traditional database tools. The information is gathered by point-of-sale systems, mobile devices, cameras, microphones, automobiles, radio-frequency identification readers, Internet searches and online tracking technologies. Popular examples are the detailed transaction data saved by retailers like Wal-Mart; the searches you conduct on Google; the "likes," "shares" and "check-ins" you post on Facebook, and the location and other information collected by smartphones and tablet devices.

Predictive analytics use a variety of techniques, from statistics, modeling and data mining, to analyze current and historical facts and then make predictions about future events. In business, patterns are sought to identify relationships among factors to guide, among other things, more effective marketing. Customer targeting is a primary objective.

A 2013 poll found that Americans are wary of both the public and the private sector when it comes to privacy protection, but are more likely to trust government entities like the Internal Revenue Service (IRS) or the National Security Agency (NSA) than for-profit companies like Facebook and Google.

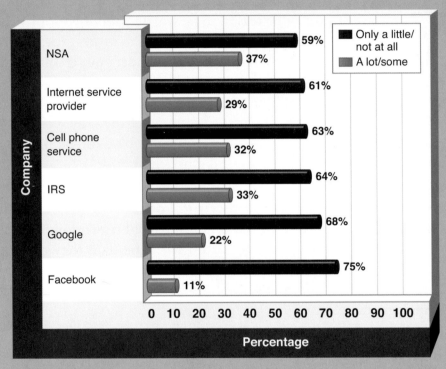

Taken from: Reason-Rupe poll, September 4–8, 2013.

Corporations Know Personal Information

Just how accurate targeting can be has been illustrated by Target. The retailer tracks the buying history and demographic information of all customers.

One way Target leverages the information is through women who sign up for its baby registry. Purchase patterns emerge, which are predictively applied to women not on the baby registry. Target then sends baby-item coupons to customers according to their pregnancy profile.

One such mailing aroused the ire of the father of a teenage girl who had received it. He complained to Target: Were they trying to encourage her to become pregnant? Shortly thereafter, he apologized to the chain, as he subsequently learned that his daughter was indeed pregnant but had been hiding it from him. Target knew the girl was pregnant before her father did.

They Know One's Race, Sexual Orientation, and More

Dynamic pricing is another common application of predictive analytics. Retailers can change the price of an item based on algorithms that include estimates of potential customers' willingness to pay. Online retailers have our personal data. They know what we've purchased, even how many times we've looked at a product. Companies are starting to use this information to figure out how much they can charge each shopper for each item.

Big Data and predictive analytics have come together to uncover hidden patterns, unknown correlations and other information that can provide organizations with new customer and business insights. Examples are numerous:

> **FAST FACT**
>
> When people go online, the Internet service provider, websites, and search engines compile data on whom they e-mail or instant message, what they search for, and what sites they read and for how long. One journalist found that 105 different companies tracked his Internet use over a thirty-six-hour period.

- Facebook "likes" can reveal, among other things, an individual's political and religious views, drug use, marital status and sexual orientation. Researchers can distinguish between Democrats and Republicans 85 percent of the time, between black and white people 95 percent of the time, and between homosexual and heterosexual men 88 percent of the time.
- Experian, Equifax and TransUnion, the big three credit-rating companies, sell demographic cluster data and home addresses to marketing firms and retailers.
- Health insurance companies buy marketing data to monitor us. Blue Cross/Blue Shield of North Carolina recently began buying

shopping data on people in its employer group plans. If someone were to buy plus-size clothing, for instance, the plan could flag them for potential obesity and therefore higher health care costs.

- Insurance companies share information with each other—your history with one company could influence the rates you pay at another for a different type of policy.
- President Barack Obama's successful 2012 campaign used a combination of massive datasets and analytical models to identify individual Republican-leaning voters who might be persuaded to vote for the president and which issues would likely trigger a switch.

You Are the Product

Governments are interested in Big Data, of course, mainly to manage the enormous volumes of information generated by their operations. But predictive analytics could be taken to an extreme as depicted in the movie "Minority Report," which had the government tracking down citizens expected to commit crimes in the future.

Still, U.S. laws prohibit governments from maintaining information on someone without cause—although national security agencies can monitor Americans with permission from a secret court—but the legal landscape generally favors business over the individual.

The United States has no universal privacy law. While federal laws protect certain sensitive information, such as medical records and financial information, there is no national law restricting online tracking. The only requirement for companies is that they disclose their practices in a privacy policy—most of which have a lot of fine print that nobody reads. States have different privacy laws. And whenever new ones are proposed, business interests lobby against them.

For the individual, understanding how things work is important. A purchase, online or in person, is a tacit agreement allowing the retailer and credit card company to collect and save data about the transaction and match it with other data they have about you.

Facebook, Twitter, Pinterest, etc. do not consider you their customer. You are their product. Their customers are advertisers. Everything you post, comment, like, tweet, or pin becomes the property of the site. It can or will be used to serve the advertisers. Each app you install might track you in some way as well.

Personal Is Not Private

There are steps you can take to enhance your privacy. For instance, you can minimize the amount of Internet tracking by enabling a "Do Not Track" feature on your web browser. Or you can turn off the GPS [Global Positioning System] feature on your phone—although this also will disable some useful features, so it's a trade-off.

Of course, as consumers we can benefit when businesses understand us. They can make us aware of products and services that better meet our needs, often at better prices than we might not otherwise find.

But remember, while your shopping history is personal, it is not private. Nor are all those things you post and click on Facebook. So conduct yourself accordingly.

EVALUATING THE AUTHOR'S ARGUMENTS:

To make his argument that companies intrusively gather data about people, viewpoint author Richard Franklin offers an example of a teenage girl who received advertising from Target. Write three or four sentences describing the situation. What was notable about the mailing the girl received? What problem does it highlight about the way in which companies track people's online behavior? Finally, state your opinion—is it acceptable that Target was able to send this mailing to this teenager? Why or why not?

Viewpoint
4

Companies Are Unlikely to Do Anything Worrisome with People's Data

David Aaronovitch

"It is possible to argue that we should be relatively unworried by data on us being held by companies."

In the following viewpoint David Aaronovitch argues that there is little reason to be suspicious of how companies use information about their customers. He acknowledges that companies collect information about people, but he does not think this is a bad or worrisome thing as they are unlikely to misuse the information or violate people's rights with it. Most information collected about people is harmless, Aaronovitch contends, and believes it is just paranoia to worry otherwise. People are social animals, he maintains; it is in their nature to want to share things about themselves and to want to learn things about others. In his opinion, this does not make them vulnerable, but rather helps them, especially because pooling information can further social, medical, and technological knowledge. Aaronovitch concludes that given the choice between keeping things private or sharing information, it is better to share information because it can benefit everyone.

Aaronovitch is a British journalist who writes a regular column for the *Times* of London.

AS YOU READ, CONSIDER THE FOLLOWING QUESTIONS:
1. What does the author say he saw on Google Street View?
2. Who is Gordon Eubanks, according to Aaronovitch?
3. What information does a cancer database discussed by the author contain?

Let me start with a story that is a sort of verbal Rorschach test [in which the test taker says the first thing that comes to mind when viewing inkblots]. I'll tell it, you see how you react to it and then we'll continue.

The year before last I decided to visit my aunt, who lives on the edge of a small country town. I hadn't been to her house before, but with the help of the AA [Automobile Association] website and by entering our postcodes I could get a detailed route plan of how to get there. But maps don't tell you everything, especially when it comes to winding lanes and disguised driveways. So I also took a look on Google Street View.

Spotting her house turned out to be difficult and I took myself digitally up and down the road several times without being able to decide where it was. And then I noticed something. Outside one house, just by its steps, was a man—his face pixellated by Google—who could only be my uncle. So that's where I drove to and that's where they were.

Differing Possible Responses

Take a moment. When you'd read that banal enough tale did you think: (a) oh, that was a bit of luck, good old Google? Or: (b) this is a chilling example of how privacy is being eroded by online information systems and databases? Well, let's see how a similar variance in outlook might translate into the bigger world. On two different evenings this week [in mid-June 2013] I encountered two almost opposite responses to the story, originally broken in [the British newspaper] *The Guardian*, concerning the information that the US National Security Agency [NSA] had been gaining from seven leading technology companies. (By the way I should note here that the story seems to have evolved from its original suggestion that the NSA simply tapped into data held by these companies, to it being that the NSA asked the companies to create a system whereby legally requested data could be copied from their own servers to its own.) On night one I was with a number of geeks and rights activists who were extremely alarmed about the idea of the NSA having the ability to "mine data" about anyone from databases created for entirely different purposes. On night two a group of centre-left friends [moderately liberal] confessed to their almost complete lack of concern. It was natural that the Government should want to use what information existed to try to track potential terrorists and crime syndicates for the good of us all. It was the ideological equivalent of spending one night in an igloo and the next in the Buri Al Arab [a posh hotel] in Dubai.

It Is Absurd to Be Suspicious of What Companies Might Do

I was talking to a well respected geek writer on Monday, one of whose arguments is that we have ceded too much personal information to others, and mostly to large corporations and the State. We may not know what the malign result is yet of our concessions, but just as a tumour may be the long-term result of behaviours, he said, so might this laxness on privacy come to haunt us.

Reading *The New York Times* this week I was struck by a quote from a veteran Silicon Valley [California, site of many high-tech companies] entrepreneur, Gordon Eubanks, who told the reporter: "I've just become really careful about what I put out there. I never put online

Silicon Valley entrepreneur Gordon Eubanks (shown) has said, "I've just become really careful about what I put out there. I never put online anything about where I live, my family, my pets. I'm even careful about what I 'like' [on Facebook]."

anything about where I live, my family, my pets. I'm even careful about what I 'like' [on Facebook]."

Nothing about his pets? What can somebody do that is harmful to him if he talks about his pets? Kidnap them, I suppose. But such carefulness seems, frankly, to be absurd. On that basis you wouldn't take your dog for a walk anywhere a dog burglar might conceivably go. Most of us have more to worry about than whether Starbucks might put our latte information to some nefarious use. Few of us want anonymity and though we like to control our self-image we are social beings and like to communicate with others.

Companies vary in the lengths they go to keep customer/user data private.

Company	Fights for users' privacy rights in Congress	Fights for users' privacy rights in courts	Publishes law enforcement guidelines	Publishes transparency reports	Tells users about government data requests	Requires a warrant for content
Amazon	X	X				
Apple	X					
AT&T	X					
Comcast		X	X			
Dropbox	X		X	X	X	X
Facebook	X		X			X
Foursquare	X		X		X	X
Google	X	X	X	X		X
LinkedIn	X		X	X	X	X
Microsoft	X		X	X		X
Myspace		X	X			X
Sonic.net	X	X	X	X	X	X
SpiderOak	X		X	X	X	X
Twitter	X	X	X	X	X	X
Tumblr	X		X	X		X
Verizon						
WordPress	X		X		X	X
Yahoo		X				

Taken from: Electronic Frontier Foundation. *Who Has Your Back?*, 2013

Issues to Consider

But it is possible to argue that we should be relatively unworried by data on us being held by companies. Back in 1999, according to *Wired* magazine, Scott McNealy, the chief executive of Sun Microsystems told Americans: "You have zero privacy. Get over it." This week, after the NSA story, the outspoken Mr McNealy was making a distinction. He asked: "Should you be afraid if AT&T [telecommunications company] has your data? Google? They're private entities. AT&T can't hurt me. Jerry Brown [the governor of California] and [President] Barack Obama can."

If I were an American I would be more likely to trust the State whose head I elect than a company over whom I can exercise no accountability other than not to buy or use a product. But there is some force to the argument that free speech may be inhibited online if you think the government might have access to it all. There is force too to the suggestion that what might feel safe under that nice Mr Obama would feel less comfortable with a [wiretapping former president Richard] Nixon in the White House. And force again to the worry that security agencies aren't quite as fabulously competent as they depict themselves.

More subtle is the worry that the fallibilities traditionally affecting enforcement agencies (confirmation bias, for example) could operate at a hugely scaled-up rate when applied to looking for patterns in vast databases. As in: "This one scores 11 out of 20 on the radicalisation index. Let's see what he does next."

Choosing Information Over Privacy

I believe that in the choice (as choice there will often be) between privacy and information, we should and we will usually choose information. But this is a mediated choice and it seems to me that the only way of adjudicating this question of what is held on us, and by whom, comes down in the end to proportionality and transparency.

On proportionality take yesterday's announcement of the database involving 11 million records of 350 cancers diagnosed across 50 million English people going back 30 years. In the wrong hands, as they say, it would be conceivably possible to identify cases. But the benefit of the database as opposed to the danger of misuse seems obvious. And I daresay the security services would say the same.

The problem is they might be wrong.

And the only way we could conceivably weigh up the risk as against the benefit is if we know what they are doing. Not in micro detail, but sufficient for us to be able to trust those who act in our names and the laws that govern their activities. If privacy is to be surrendered then the price of our transparency is theirs. Without it, the deal won't work.

EVALUATING THE AUTHOR'S ARGUMENTS:

David Aaronovitch (this viewpoint's author) and Richard Franklin (author of the previous viewpoint) disagree on whether companies can be trusted with people's private information. After reading both viewpoints, what is your opinion on this issue? Are you comfortable with companies knowing private details about you? Why or why not? Support your answer with at least one piece of information from the texts you have read.

Social Media Threaten Privacy

Bruce Schneier

"If the National Security Agency required us to notify it whenever we made a new friend, the nation would rebel. Yet we notify Facebook."

In the following viewpoint Bruce Schneier argues that social media use threatens privacy. He discusses how a rare and threatening partnership has arisen between the government, which seeks private information for security purposes, and corporations, which seek personal information for marketing purposes. He explains that the government wants to collect information so it can ostensibly prevent terrorist attacks. It therefore has no incentive to limit or regulate data collection, which corporations take advantage of to more precisely sell their products. Add to this mix social media users who ignorantly divulge their preferences, hobbies, and personal details online, and Schneier maintains that the result is a critical loss of privacy that threatens every American. Schneier concludes that although social media use may seem harmless, it furthers corporate and state goals that do little to benefit American citizens.

Schneier is a computer security technology expert who writes frequently on the issues of privacy and technology.

AS YOU READ, CONSIDER THE FOLLOWING QUESTIONS:
  1. To whom does Schneier say we willingly provide copies of our text messages and e-mails?
  2. What is the difference between constitutional law and regulatory law, according to Schneier?
  3. To what does the phrase "incestuous relationship" refer, as used by the author?

I magine the government passed a law requiring all citizens to carry a tracking device. Such a law would immediately be found unconstitutional. Yet we all carry mobile phones.

If the National Security Agency [NSA] required us to notify it whenever we made a new friend, the nation would rebel. Yet we notify Facebook Inc. If the Federal Bureau of Investigation demanded copies of all our conversations and correspondence, it would be laughed at. Yet we provide copies of our e-mail to Google Inc., Microsoft Corp. or whoever our mail host is; we provide copies of our text messages to Verizon Communications Inc., AT&T Inc. and Sprint Corp.; and we provide copies of other conversations to Twitter Inc., Facebook, LinkedIn Corp. or whatever other site is hosting them.

The Internet's Business Model Is Built on Mass Surveillance

The primary business model of the Internet is built on mass surveillance, and our government's intelligence-gathering agencies have become addicted to that data. Understanding how we got here is critical to understanding how we undo the damage.

Computers and networks inherently produce data, and our constant interactions with them allow corporations to collect an enormous amount of intensely personal data about us as we go about our daily lives. Sometimes we produce this data inadvertently simply by using our phones, credit cards, computers and other devices. Sometimes we give corporations this data directly on Google, Facebook, Apple Inc.'s iCloud and so on in exchange for whatever free or cheap service we receive from the Internet in return.

The NSA is also in the business of spying on everyone, and it has realized it's far easier to collect all the data from these corporations rather than from us directly. In some cases, the NSA asks for this data nicely. In other cases, it makes use of subtle threats or overt pressure. If that doesn't work, it uses tools like national security letters [which order a company to turn over its records in matters of national security].

Americans may be concerned with privacy issues online, yet many tell their secrets on Facebook, which can be just as damaging.

A Surveillance Partnership

The result is a corporate-government surveillance partnership, one that allows both the government and corporations to get away with things they couldn't otherwise.

There are two types of laws in the U.S., each designed to constrain a different type of power: constitutional Law, which places limitations on government, and regulatory law, which constrains corporations.

Historically, these two areas have largely remained separate, but today each group has learned how to use the other's laws to bypass their own restrictions. The government uses corporations to get around its limits, and corporations use the government to get around their limits.

This partnership manifests itself in various ways. The government uses corporations to circumvent its prohibitions against eavesdropping domestically on its citizens. Corporations rely on the government to ensure that they have unfettered use of the data they collect.

Here's an example: It would be reasonable for our government to debate the circumstances under which corporations can collect and use our data, and to provide for protections against misuse. But if the government is using that very data for its own surveillance purposes, it has an incentive to oppose any laws to limit data collection. And because corporations see no need to give consumers any choice in this matter—because it would only reduce their profits—the market isn't going to protect consumers, either.

Our elected officials are often supported, endorsed and funded by these corporations as well, setting up an incestuous relationship between corporations, lawmakers and the intelligence community.

Everyone Loses When Privacy Dies

The losers are us, the people, who are left with no one to stand up for our interests. Our elected government, which is supposed to be

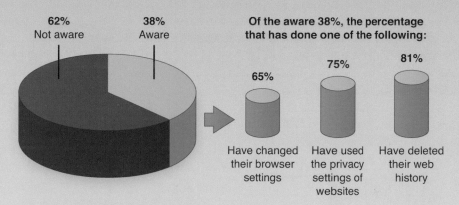

Americans Do Not Know How to Protect Their Privacy Online

Fewer than half of those polled knew ways to limit how much personal information websites collect about them.

62% Not aware	38% Aware	Of the aware 38%, the percentage that has done one of the following:

65% — Have changed their browser settings

75% — Have used the privacy settings of websites

81% — Have deleted their web history

Taken from: Pew Internet & American Life Project, 2012.

responsible to us, is not. And corporations, which in a market economy are supposed to be responsive to our needs, are not. What we have now is death to privacy—and that's very dangerous to democracy and liberty.

The simple answer is to blame consumers, who shouldn't use mobile phones, credit cards, banks or the Internet if they don't want to be tracked. But that argument deliberately ignores the reality of today's world. Everything we do involves computers, even if we're not using them directly. And by their nature, computers produce tracking data. We can't go back to a world where we don't use computers, the Internet or social networking. We have no choice but to share our personal information with these corporations/because that's how our world works today.

Curbing the power of the corporate-private surveillance partnership requires limitations on both what corporations can do with the data we choose to give them and restrictions on how and when the government can demand access to that data. Because both of these changes go against the interests of corporations and the government, we have to demand them as citizens and voters. We can lobby our government to operate more transparently—disclosing the opinions of the Foreign Intelligence Surveillance Court [which grants permission, in secret, for government to access personal data] would be a good start—and hold our lawmakers accountable when it doesn't. But it's not going to be easy. There are strong interests doing their best to ensure that the steady stream of data keeps flowing.

EVALUATING THE AUTHOR'S ARGUMENTS:

In this viewpoint Bruce Schneier points out that Americans would never tolerate being required to wear a tracking device or to turn over their communications to the government—but they are more than willing to voluntarily do these things via their use of social media. What do you think? Is having a smartphone the equivalent of wearing a tracking device? Is sending text messages, using Twitter, or having an e-mail account the equivalent of turning over copies of your communications to corporations? Explain your thoughts on this issue and support your answer with examples from the texts you have read.

Social Media Do Not Threaten Privacy

> "It is rarely the social media company that invades your privacy. What haunts people is typically user-generated content."

Lothar Determann

Social media do not violate personal privacy, argues Lothar Determann in the following viewpoint. He also argues that understandings of personal privacy are deeply flawed; rights to privacy are vague and undefined and cannot reasonably be said to apply to a corporate context. Furthermore, says Determann, social media deals in information that users provide about themselves. Therefore, says Determann, social media users are the ones violating their own privacy, not the social media companies. If people do not want their private information accessible, then they should not post it, he opines. Determann concludes that social media companies cannot be blamed for providing a service that people willingly use.

Determann practices international technology, commercial, and intellectual property law and teaches these subjects at the University of California–Berkeley School of Law and Hastings College of the Law in San Francisco.

AS YOU READ, CONSIDER THE FOLLOWING QUESTIONS:
1. What do constitutional rights to privacy *not* protect people against, according to the author?
2. What is "user-generated content," as described by Determann?
3. How many active users did Facebook have as of December 31, 2011, according to Determann?

Expectations of data privacy and privacy rights tend to be grossly exaggerated these days. Fact is that most constitutions and international human rights treaties do not explicitly recognize rights to privacy. Even if you find privacy rights in constitutions, expressly or impliedly, constitutional rights protect you directly only against governments and state actors, but not typically against companies or individual social media users. Where courts refer to constitutional or other privacy rights, they have to balance them against other civil rights. In the social media context, privacy interests are often pitched directly against rights to free speech and information. Communication freedoms generally trump privacy rights because the rights to free speech and information have been explicitly acknowledged in constitutions and human rights treaties around the world for centuries, and they have been recognized to afford particularly robust protections for media companies.

Another reason why privacy expectations directed at social media companies tend to be misguided is that in the social media context, it is rarely the social media company that invades your privacy. What haunts people is typically user-generated content, i.e., information that people themselves, their friends, and other social media users upload. If other social media users disseminate offensive information, you may have claims against them under tort laws against libel and invasion of privacy. But, social media platform providers are not directly responsible for user generated privacy invasions. They can claim broad exemptions from contributory liability under existing laws that were intended to protect Internet service providers. . . .

Posts Belong to the Company

Talk about informational self-determination and proposals for property law regimes to protect privacy sometimes gives people the idea that they own personal data about themselves. Fact is that no one owns facts. Factual information is largely excluded from intellectual property law protection: copyright law protects only creative expression, not factual information. Trade secret law protects information that companies keep secret if such information derives an economic value from being secret. Personal information about you that you or others post on social media platforms, however, is not secret and thus not subject to trade secret law protection. When social media companies aggregate information about usage and user preferences, the social media companies can claim trade secret ownership rights in such aggregate information, but they own such trade secrets and you do not. Also, databases with content and personal information can be protected under European database laws and U.S. state laws on appropriation, but again, as property of the social media companies and not as your personal property. So, if anyone owns personal data about you, it is the social media companies, not you. . . .

Do Not Blame the Social Media Companies

Some people attribute whatever privacy intrusion occurs in a social media context to the companies that operate the networks. Fact is that some social media companies have had to settle privacy related lawsuits and charges. Missteps are part of growing pains of any new industry, particularly one driven by new technologies and start-up companies operating in a rapidly developing legal environment. In [some] cases . . . , social media companies were primarily charged because of data security weaknesses and failure to provide sufficiently conspicuous notices when prompting consumers to consent to changes. Data security and consumer consent requirements have been in flux for years and companies in many industries have been struggling to keep up or catch up with the law. It is no surprise that social media companies have also had difficulties clearing compliance hurdles as the bars are being raised.

There is no reason, however, to take such missteps as an indication that social media companies constitute a systematic threat to privacy. Social media companies are strongly incentivized to avoid harming users or prospective users. They are operated for profit and have to cater to user demands. Social media companies create technology platforms and offer features that users demand. Most privacy threats in the social media sphere have emanated from the manner in which people have used social media platforms. Social media companies do not select or post any harmful information. Individual users add the personal data. If users cannot be social and share data on social media platforms, then they will disseminate information in person, over the phone, on Internet blogs, and elsewhere. The urge of individuals to be social and share information is what has the greatest effect on privacy. It is a myth that social media companies are to blame for this.

Targeted Advertising Does Not Violate Privacy

Activists, academics and regulators are quite discontented with tracking, profiling and behavioral advertising. The practices are also not particularly popular with users who understand them. But can they really be perceived as a significant threat to privacy? Where is the harm? All that advertisers want is to display more relevant advertisements to consumers. That in itself is hardly a bad thing. Relevant advertisements are better than irrelevant advertisements. Some consumers might prefer seeing no advertisements at all, or relevant advertisements without tracking. These options are not available in practice, though. Advertisers need tracking information to target ads, and social media companies need funding from advertisers in order to offer services free of charge to consumers. Without advertising dollars, Internet companies could never have created all the services that we have come to enjoy and depend on in our daily lives, including web search, maps and social media. Governments could not have created them with taxpayer money and paid services are much less quickly adopted and usually only on the heels of charge-free services. Most consumers are more or less aware of the trade-off and the fact that they pay for services with their data and willingness to endure ads. They are also quite willing

Consumers Are Willing to Accept That Companies Will Use Their Data

Many consumers are either very or somewhat comfortable with the fact that companies use their data, though they do not trust all companies equally.

Question: *"How comfortable are you, if at all, about your privacy and the use of these data?"*

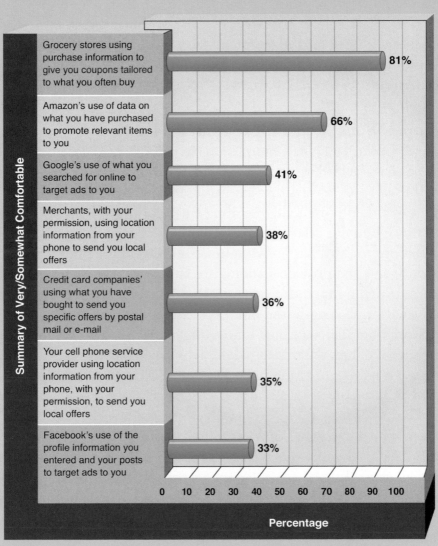

Summary of Very/Somewhat Comfortable

Category	Percentage
Grocery stores using purchase information to give you coupons tailored to what you often buy	81%
Amazon's use of data on what you have purchased to promote relevant items to you	66%
Google's use of what you searched for online to target ads to you	41%
Merchants, with your permission, using location information from your phone to send you local offers	38%
Credit card companies' using what you have bought to send you specific offers by postal mail or e-mail	36%
Your cell phone service provider using location information from your phone, with your permission, to send you local offers	35%
Facebook's use of the profile information you entered and your posts to target ads to you	33%

Percentage

Taken from: PlaceCast, "The Alert Shopper III: How Consumers Really Feel About Data Privacy," 2012.

to allow tracking offline. For example, shoppers routinely let retailers build extensive profiles on their consumption habits in return for a small discount. Of course, it is possible that user profiles built by advertisers can be abused by others. For example, health insurance companies and employers could use information in user profiles to discriminate against sick people if they gain access; but, such threats to privacy emanate primarily from the practices of health insurance companies and employers. Such concerns should be—and are—addressed in insurance regulations and labor laws. Another group of commonly cited examples relates to fears regarding abuse of user profiles by criminals and governments. Such fears also do not support attempts to cast advertisers as the primary threat to privacy, because criminals and governments play the lead role in these horror stories and point to solutions in the form of stricter laws on data security and government access. . . .

People Want Media More than Privacy

The U.S. Federal Trade Commission has publicly filed complaints and stated that the leading social media platform operators have handled their users' data in ways that harmed users by threatening their health and safety and potentially revealing their political views, sexual orientation, business relationships, and other sensitive information and affiliations to third parties without authorization. The press reported extensively. The providers apologized and settled the charges without putting up much of a defense. They continue the push for more information sharing in the interest of expanding the reach of social networks and they continue innovating and expanding the commercialization of user data. Meanwhile, active social media user numbers are reaching record highs: as of December 31, 2011, Facebook had 845 million monthly active users, a 39 percent increase as compared to the same figure a year earlier; Twitter experienced a 182 percent increase in the number of its mobile users between early 2010 and early 2011, all while the average number of Tweets per day nearly tripled; as of January 2012, Google+ amassed over 90 million registered users since launching just half a year earlier. The consumers have spoken: they are not concerned. People care more about getting free media than they do about their privacy.

EVALUATING THE AUTHOR'S ARGUMENTS:

In this viewpoint Lothar Determann argues that if people do not like the privacy implications that come along with using social media and the Internet, they should not use such technologies. What would Bruce Schneier, author of the previous viewpoint, say in response to this argument? Write two or three sentences on what you think Schneier might say; then state with which author you agree, and why.

Facts About Privacy

Editor's note: These facts can be used in reports to add credibility when making important points or claims.

Privacy and Technology

According to the American Civil Liberties Union:

- The Electronic Communications Privacy Act (ECPA), which protects people's private messages, was written in 1986 and should be updated to include e-mail, the Internet, and other technologies that have been introduced since then.
- On a typical day,
    - more than 50 percent of American adults use the Internet;
    - more than 40 percent send or receive e-mail;
    - at least 35 percent use a search engine;
    - about 25 percent read the news online;
    - more than 10 percent use a social networking site;
    - more than 15 percent use online banking services; and
    - about 10 percent watch videos.
- Eighty-nine percent of Americans aged eighteen to twenty-nine who go online watch videos on video-sharing sites—predominantly, YouTube.
- Sixty-nine percent of adults who go online use cloud computing services to create, send, receive, or store documents.
- More than 70 percent of young people and 35 percent of adults who go online have a profile on a social networking site.
- Eighty-three percent of Americans own a cell phone, and 35 percent of them have accessed the Internet on their phone.
- Thirty-four percent store photos online.
- These services offer benefits, but they also can learn a user's interests and associations by tracking their Internet searches, e-mails, cloud computing documents, photos, social networking activities, e-books, and videos.

A 2012 Pew Internet & American Life Project study found that
- 75 percent of teens text;
- the median number of texts sent and received on a typical day by Americans aged twelve to seventeen increased from fifty in 2009 to sixty in 2011.
- girls aged fourteen to seventeen text most often, with a median of one hundred texts a day in 2011, whereas boys the same age sent fifty texts;
- 63 percent of teens send text messages daily while using other forms of daily communication, including calling on a cell phone (39 percent), face-to-face socializing outside of school (35 percent), social networking (29 percent), instant messaging (22 percent), talking on landlines (19 percent), and e-mailing (6 percent); and
- 18 percent of smartphone owners have shared their location by "checking in" online.

A Pew Research Center study of Internet users in 2013 showed that
- 68 percent of Americans say current laws do not do enough to protect privacy;
- 86 percent of Americans have taken steps to cover up their online activity, such as clearing their cookies or encrypting their e-mail;
- 55 percent have taken steps online to avoid detection by specific people, organizations, or the government;
- 21 percent say their e-mail or social networking account has been hacked or taken over by someone without permission;
- 12 percent have experienced cyberstalking or harassment online;
- 11 percent have had their Social Security number, credit card, or bank account information stolen;
- 6 percent have lost money in an online scam;
- 6 percent have had their reputation damaged because of something that happened online; and
- 4 percent have been led into physical danger because of online activities.

Privacy and Surveillance
According to a National Security Agency (NSA) presentation made public in 2013, during a typical day, the NSA collects
- 444,743 e-mail address books from Yahoo;
- 105,068 from Hotmail;

- 82,857 from Facebook;
- 33,697 from Gmail;
- 22,881 from other providers;
- a total of more than 250 million e-mail address books a year;
- 500,000 buddy lists on live-chat services, which include offline messages and messages waiting to be delivered, and show the first few lines of unread inbox messages.

A 2013 *Washington Post*/ABC News poll showed that
- 57 percent of Americans think it is important for the federal government to investigate terrorism, even if it must intrude on personal privacy;
- 39 percent believe the government should not infringe on privacy, even if that limits its investigation of terrorism; and
- 74 percent think that the government's collection of phone and Internet records violates some Americans' right to privacy, while only 22 percent think it does not;
    - of those who think it violates privacy rights, 39 percent think that it is justified, while 55 percent say that it is not;
- 49 percent fear that the government's surveillance of phone calls and web usage intrudes on their own privacy rights, while 44 percent say it does not;
    - of those who believe it infringes on privacy rights, just 28 percent say it is justified, while 70 percent think it is not;
- when asked whether the NSA's surveillance program is making the United States safer from terrorism, 42 percent say it is, 5 percent say it actually makes the country less safe, and 47 percent say it is not making a difference.

According to a Study by Rand Europe in 2010:
- People are becoming more comfortable walking through X-ray or body scanners, seeing them as less invasive than undergoing a physical pat-down or bag search; however, detectors or scanning machines are actually more invasive of privacy than X-rays since their images are seen by multiple people at a time and potentially recorded and shared later.
- To feel secure while attending a major public event, people preferred to have their identity checked before entering and were willing to pay for these measures; however, they were unlikely

to pay for checks that required private biometric data, such as fingerprints.

- Under the Patriot Act, government agencies can secretly request data on US citizens and visitors even if they are not the subject of a criminal investigation.
- Privacy studies show that people can be categorized as one of the following:
    - privacy fundamentalists (about 25 percent of the US population)—people who generally distrust organizations that ask for personal information and worry about the accuracy of electronic data.
    - Privacy pragmatists (57 percent of Americans)—people who consider the benefits of consumer opportunities and public safety before they decide whether to give up their personal data.
    - privacy unconcerned (about 18 percent)—those who generally trust organizations that compile their personal data and are willing to forgo privacy for security or consumer benefits.

Consumer Privacy/Companies' Use of Private Data

A survey by Evidon and Dynamic Logic in 2011 found that

- 50 percent of consumers like having online ads targeted toward them on the basis of their interests but have a strong desire to know how they are being targeted;
- 76 percent want to know the identities of all companies involved in ads targeted to them;
- 57 percent feel more positive toward brands that tell them exactly how they are being targeted;
- 67 percent prefer brands that give them more control of their data and the ability to opt out; and
- 36 percent report that this kind of transparency increases the likelihood that they will buy from a brand.

According to the 2012 White House report *Consumer Data Privacy in a Networked World*:

- The first Fair Information Practice Principles (FIPPs) were set in 1973, when the government outlined "safeguard requirements" for Americans' personal data.

- The Consumer Privacy Bill of Rights proposed by President Barack Obama builds on the FIPPs; it covers commercial uses of personal data, which is data linkable to a specific individual, computer, smartphone, or other device.
- The Consumer Privacy Bill of Rights says all consumers have the following rights:
    - to exercise control over what personal data companies collect from them and how they use it;
    - to easily access understandable information about privacy and security practices;
    - to have their personal data collected and used in ways that they would reasonably expect;
    - to have secure, responsible handling of their personal information;
    - to access and correct their personal data;
    - to have reasonable limits placed on the data that companies retain; and
    - to have their personal information handled by companies that adhere to the Consumer Privacy Bill of Rights.

According to a privacy report of the Federal Trade Commission (FTC) in 2012, the FTC
- filed complaints against Google and Facebook that resulted in orders that protect over a billion users globally; both companies must obtain users' consent before changing privacy practices, which will be subject to review by auditors for twenty years;
- charged that Google had used private information of Gmail users to populate its social network, Google Buzz, which made some people's most frequent e-mail contacts public.

Organizations to Contact

The editors have compiled the following list of organizations concerned with the issues debated in this book. The descriptions are derived from materials provided by the organizations. All have publications or information available for interested readers. The list was compiled on the date of publication of the present volume; the information provided here may change. Be aware that many organizations take several weeks or longer to respond to inquiries, so allow as much time as possible for the receipt of requested materials.

American Civil Liberties Union (ACLU)
125 Broad St., 18th Fl.
New York, NY 10004-2400
(212) 549-2500
e-mail: aclu@aclu.org
website: www.aclu.org

The ACLU is a national organization that works to defend Americans' civil rights guaranteed by the US Constitution. It argues daily in courts, legislatures, and communities to preserve individual liberties, such as freedom of speech, freedom of the press, and privacy rights. Following the September 2001 terrorist attacks on the United States, the ACLU founded its National Security Project, which litigates national security cases involving discrimination, torture, detention, surveillance, and secrecy, to protect every human's fundamental rights.

American Enterprise Institute for Public Policy Research (AEI)
1150 Seventeenth St. NW
Washington, DC 20036
(202) 862-5800 • fax: (202) 862-7177
e-mail: aei@aei.org
website: www.aei.org

The AEI is a private nonprofit, conservative think tank dedicated to research and education on issues of government, politics, economics, and social welfare. It provides policy makers with ideas to meet today's challenges on the basis of the principles of private liberty, free enterprise, and individual opportunity. The AEI's Legal Center for the Public Interest focuses on constitutional research in an effort to preserve the liberties guaranteed in the Constitution. Many of its publications deal with the issue of privacy.

CATO Institute
1000 Massachusetts Ave. NW
Washington, DC 20001-5403
(202) 842-0200 • fax: (202) 842-3490
e-mail: cato@cato.org
website: www.cato.org

Founded in 1977, the institute is a nonpartisan, nonprofit libertarian public policy research foundation dedicated to limiting the role of government and protecting individual liberties. It publishes the quarterly magazine *Regulation*, the bimonthly *Cato Policy Report*, and numerous policy papers and articles, including many focused on privacy and security issues.

Center for Democracy & Technology (CDT)
1634 Eye St. NW, #1100
Washington, DC 20006
(202) 637-9800 • fax: (202) 637-0968
e-mail: webmaster@cdt.org
website: www.cdt.org

The CDT is a nonprofit public interest organization that develops public policy solutions that advance democratic values in all communications media. With expertise in law, technology, and policy, its mission is to keep the Internet open, innovative, and free and to ensure that privacy and free expression are promoted in all communications technologies. Its publications include issue briefs, testimony and speeches, many of which focus on privacy-related issues.

Electronic Frontier Foundation (EFF)
815 Eddy St.
San Francisco, CA 94109
(415) 436-9333 • fax: (415) 436-9993
e-mail: information@eff.org
website: www.eff.org

Founded in 1990, the EFF is a nonprofit watchdog organization that defends civil liberties such as privacy on the Internet. EFF blends the expertise of policy analysts, lawyers, technologists, and activists to confront threats to free speech, privacy, innovation, and intellectual property and consumer rights in the digital world. It produces a number of white papers on privacy and the Internet, all of which are available through its website.

Electronic Privacy Information Center (EPIC)
1718 Connecticut Ave. NW, Ste. 200
Washington, DC 20009
(202) 483-1140 • fax: (202) 483-1248
website: http://epic.org

Established in 1994, EPIC is a public-interest research center devoted to researching emerging civil liberties issues, privacy, the First Amendment, and constitutional values in the electronic age. EPIC publishes reports and books about privacy, open government, free speech, and other important topics, as well as annual reports and the *EPIC Alert*, an online newsletter.

The Freedom Forum
555 Pennsylvania Ave. NW
Washington, DC 20001
(202) 292-6100
e-mail: news@freedomforum.org
website: www.freedomforum.org

The Freedom Forum is a nonpartisan foundation that works to protect free press, free speech, and free spirit for all people. Freedom Forum focuses its attention on three areas, Newseum, an interactive museum of news in Washington, DC; the First Amendment Center, and the

Diversity Institute. Together, they aim to monitor developments in media and First Amendment issues.

Human Rights Watch
350 Fifth Ave., 34th Fl.
New York, NY 10118-3299
(212) 290-4700 • fax: (212) 736-1300
e-mail: hrwnyc@hrw.org
website: www.hrw.org

Human Rights Watch is an independent organization that regularly investigates human rights abuses in more than seventy countries around the world and holds violators of these rights accountable. It works to lay the legal and moral groundwork to defend and protect human rights for all while also promoting civil liberties and defending freedom of thought, due process, and equal protection of the law. It publishes the *Human Rights Watch Quarterly Newsletter* and the annual *Human Rights Watch World Report.*

Institute for Justice
901 N. Glebe Rd., Ste. 900
Arlington, VA 22203
(703) 682-9320 • fax: (703) 682-9321
e-mail: general@ij.org
website: www.ij.org

The Institute for Justice is a libertarian public-interest law firm providing litigation and advocacy on behalf of individuals whose most basic rights have been violated by the government. It works to secure privacy rights for all members of society and aims to restore constitutional limits on the power of government. Among its publications are *Liberty & Law,* a bimonthly newsletter; various reports; articles; and papers on various privacy issues.

National Security Agency (NSA)
9800 Savage Rd.
Ft. George Meade, MD 20755
(301) 688-6524 • fax: (301) 688-6198
website: www.nsa.gov

The NSA is a cryptologic agency (i.e., one that deciphers codes) administered by the US Department of Defense. Its main goal is to protect national security systems and to produce foreign intelligence information. The NSA follows US laws to defeat terrorist organizations at home and abroad and ensures the protection of privacy and civil liberties of American citizens. Speeches, congressional testimonies, press releases, and research reports are all available on the NSA website. It is at the heart of many of the debates about privacy and security.

US Department of Homeland Security (DHS)
Washington, DC 20528
(202) 282-8000
website: www.dhs.gov

The DHS was created after the September 11, 2001, terrorist attacks. The department serves to secure the nation while preserving American freedoms and liberties. It is charged with protecting the United States from terrorists, decreasing the country's vulnerability to terrorism, and effectively responding to attacks. It is a key organization in debates on privacy and security.

Martin, Rhodri. "Snoop Away—We've Gone Too Far to Turn Back," *Independent* (London), June 7, 2013.

Robinson, Eugene. "Is Privacy Dead?," *Newsday*, June 7, 2013.

Schneier, Bruce. "The Internet Is a Surveillance State," CNN.com, March 16, 2013.

Troni, Naomi. "Social Media Privacy: A Contradiction in Terms?," *Forbes*, April 24, 2012.

Wellington, Beth. "What Facebook Fails to Recognise," *Guardian* (Manchester, UK), June 14, 2011.

Websites

Digital Due Process (http://digitaldueprocess.org). This website explores the issue of digital privacy. It argues that the Electronic Communications Privacy Act (ECPA), written in 1986, needs to be updated to reflect technology of today.

Privacy Foundation (www.law.du.edu/index.php/privacy-foundation). A good resource for cases and news briefs relating to all kinds of privacy issues, including medical privacy, private property, identity theft, student privacy, and more.

Privacy International (www.privacyinternational.org). This site reports on the secret world of government surveillance and exposes the companies enabling it. The website contains fact sheets and videos about numerous ongoing projects.

Privacy Rights Clearinghouse (www.privacyrights.org). A nonprofit consumer education and advocacy project whose purpose is to advocate for consumers' privacy rights in public policy proceedings. The website contains numerous articles and fact sheets on privacy in a variety of settings.

Index

Americans should trade some, for increased security, 41–46

choice between information and, 87

is dead, 12–18

is not dead, 19–23

is overrated, 34–39

is underrated, 24–33

online, case against, 71–75

should not be sacrificed for technological convenience, 66–70

social media threaten, 89–94

stems consumers can take to enhance, 81

Supreme Court first recognizes right of, 36

Privacy law(s)

are paternalistic, 36

do not protect user-provided personal information, 96–97

in Europe, 29, 69

need to be updated, 64

US lacks universal, 80

S

Schneier, Bruce, 25, *27,* 89

September 11 attacks (2001), *14,* 48

new norms following, 16–18

repeat of, would end civil liberties, 42–43

Simon, David, 44–45, 46

Smith v. Maryland (1979), 57, 63

Snowden, Edward, 14, 17, 18, *43*

is not whistle-blower, 43–44

support for criminal prosecution of, 15

Social media

do not threaten privacy, 95–101

threaten privacy, 89–94

Solove, Daniel J., 24

Solzhenitsyn, Aleksandr, 26

Stanley, Jay, 60

Stone, Geoffrey, 25

Stored Communications Act (1986), 84

Street View (Google)

European limitations on, 69

lawsuits against, 15

Sullivan, Andrew, 44

Supreme Court, 35

on protection and respect of privacy, 57

on limitations on privacy rights, 63–64

rules on privacy as constitutional right, 35

Surveillance cameras, 35, 37–39

Surveys

of adults on use of Internet, *56*

on approval of government data collecting, 57, 62

on ways used to protect privacy online, 20, *22, 93*

on importance of government's antiterrorism efforts and, 15, 44, *45*

on personal information of adult Internet users available online, *30*

on prevalence of linking
cells phone to personal
accounts, 72
on privacy concerns about
companies using consumer
data, *99*
on steps Americans take to
protect privacy, 20
on support for government's
security measures, *38*
on use of Facebook privacy
settings, 97

deaths of Americans by guns
vs., 52
views on importance of
government's actions to
prevent, 15, 44, *45*
Twitter, 15, 80
measures taken by, to protect
consumer data, *86*
number of users of, 100

Picture Credits

© AP Images/Ed Andrieski, 58

© AP Images/Facebook, Alan Brandt, 65

© AP Images/Ann Heisenfelt, 27

© AP Images/Kyodo, 73

© Adam Berry/ Bloomberg via Getty Images, 37

© Victor Biro/Alamy, 50

© Cengage, Gale, 22, 30, 38, 45, 52, 56, 78, 86, 93, 99

© Lucie Lang/Alamy, 21

© Laperrugue/Alamy, 14

© John Moore/Getty Images, 40

© Vladimir Nenov/Alamy, 11

© Sunshinepress/Getty Images, 43

© Urbanmyth/Alamy, 91

© Jim Urquhart/Reuters/Landov, 63

© Ann E. Yow-Dyson/Getty Images, 85